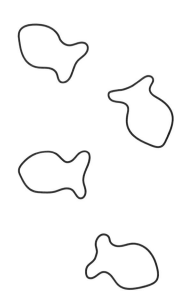

THE MOM LIFE

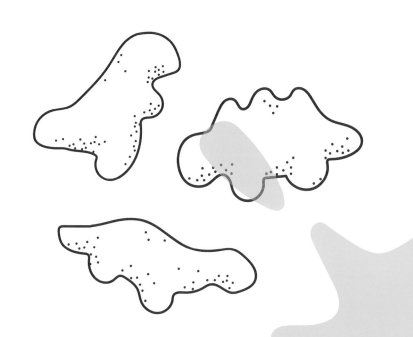

THE MOM LIFE

The Sweet, the Bitter, and the Bittersweet Fruits of Motherhood

LINDA FRUITS

VORACIOUS

Little, Brown and Company
New York / Boston / London

Voracious / Little, Brown and Company
Hachette Book Group
1290 Avenue of the Americas, New York, NY 10104
littlebrown.com

First Edition: March 2023

Voracious is an imprint of Little, Brown and Company, a division of Hachette Book Group, Inc.
The Voracious name and logo are trademarks of Hachette Book Group, Inc.

The publisher is not responsible for websites (or their content) that are not owned by the
publisher.

The Hachette Speakers Bureau provides a wide range of authors for speaking events.
To find out more, go to hachettespeakersbureau.com or email hachettespeakers@hbgusa.com.

Little, Brown and Company books may be purchased in bulk for business, educational, or
promotional use. For information, please contact your local bookseller or the Hachette Book
Group Special Markets Department at special.markets@hbgusa.com.

ISBN 9780316437004
LCCN 2022939725

Printing 1, 2022

LSC-C

Printed in the United States of America

This book is dedicated to my mom, who never placed any unrealistic expectations on me as a mother—I did that.

And to every mother: you inspire me to accept the mom I am and not the mom I thought I was going to be.

Together we are changing the collective narrative of what it means to be a mother.

CONTENTS

Introduction 11

1 You have to **FUCK** up 22

2 **LOVE** can take time 32

3 You are not required to **BOUNCE** back 40

4 I do…not remember **HATING** my partner 50

5 It's okay to have **ZERO** sexual appetite 60

6 Fed is best, **STILL** 70

7 WTF are **PPA** and PPD? 80

8 I didn't ask, so **DON'T** tell 92

9 If it ain't broken…um, **BREAK** it 98

10 If you have a baby, you **ARE** a mama 108

11 There will be **CRYING...** 114

12 All the **FEELS** 122

13 You can't and **SHOULDN'T** do it all 128

14 You are hereby found **NOT GUILTY** 136

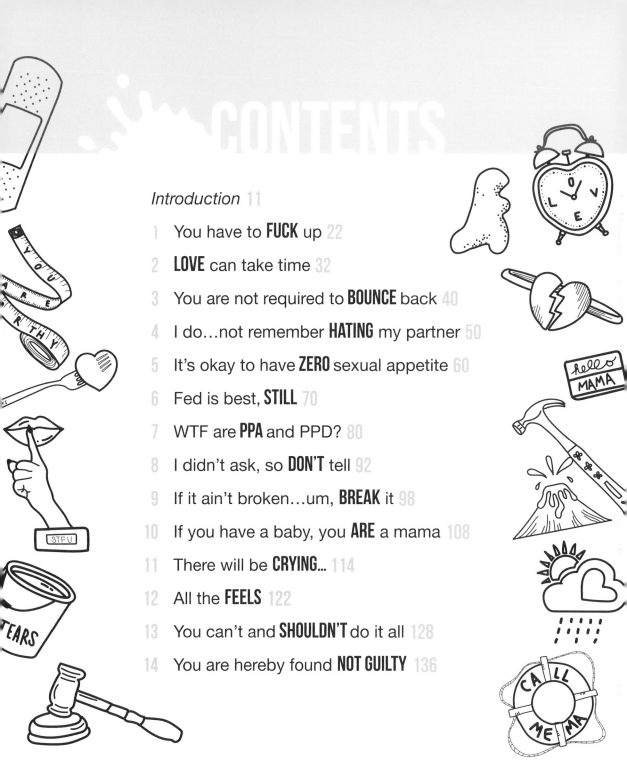

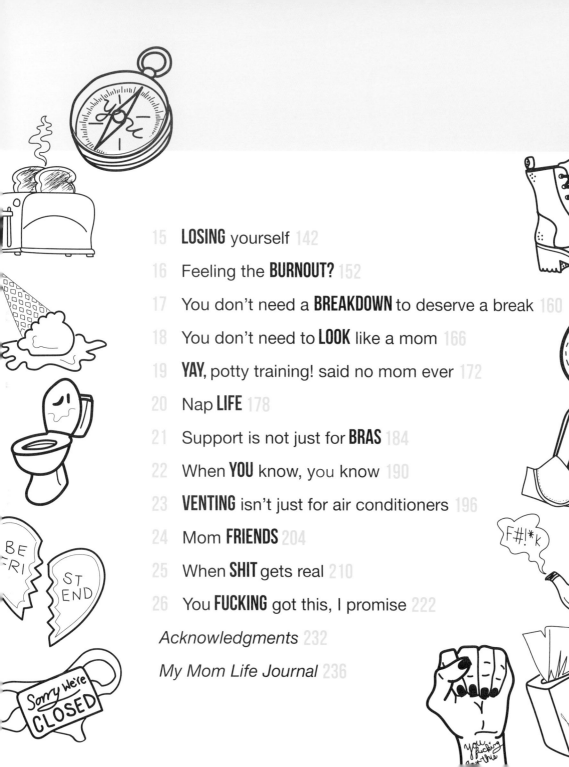

15 **LOSING** yourself 142

16 Feeling the **BURNOUT?** 152

17 You don't need a **BREAKDOWN** to deserve a break 160

18 You don't need to **LOOK** like a mom 166

19 **YAY,** potty training! said no mom ever 172

20 Nap **LIFE** 178

21 Support is not just for **BRAS** 184

22 When **YOU** know, you know 190

23 **VENTING** isn't just for air conditioners 196

24 Mom **FRIENDS** 204

25 When **SHIT** gets real 210

26 You **FUCKING** got this, I promise 222

Acknowledgments 232

My Mom Life Journal 236

Sometimes

Sometimes you'll feel like a failure.

Sometimes you'll count down the minutes 'til you get a minute alone.

Sometimes you'll wonder why you decided to procreate in the first place.

Sometimes you'll wonder what you're doing wrong.

Sometimes you'll wonder why you feel so alone.

Sometimes you'll wonder if the house will ever be clean again.

Sometimes you'll wonder what happened to your body.

Sometimes you'll hate being a mom.

But then sometimes you'll love it.

Sometimes you'll love the way their eyes glisten when they see you.

Sometimes their laughter will be better than the Sweet Vanilla Cream Cold Brew from Starbucks.

Sometimes the way they sleep will make you cry.

Sometimes you'll love the way they give you sloppy kisses.

Sometimes you'll want a moment to last a lifetime.

Sometimes you'll stand back and feel overjoyed by the life you've made.

Sometimes you'll wonder how you ever survived without them.

INTRODUCTION

Introduction

You may be thinking that because I wrote a book on motherhood, I've got it all figured out…. I hate to break it to you, but no one does. What I do have figured out is that moms need a new set of standards. We're constantly bombarded with the unachievable: aka needing to be perfect. I want to destigmatize and normalize the parts of motherhood most of us probably don't want to admit to: like not wanting to have sex with our partners for months (or years) after a baby is born. That it is okay to make mistakes. That love can take time. I want to show us all how to handle losing ourselves. But ultimately, I want to reassure every mom.

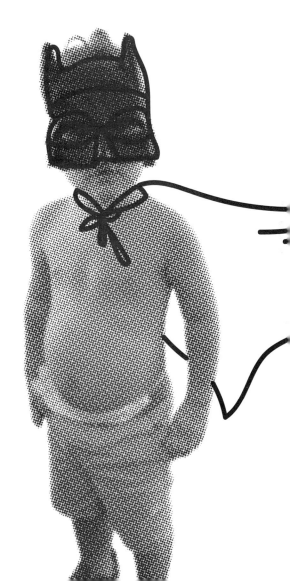

I promise: you fucking got this.

WE'RE NOT PERFECT IN ANY OTHER ASPECT OF LIFE — WHY SHOULD WE EXPECT PERFECTION IN MOTHERHOOD?

So, who the hell is Linda Fruits? I'm one of those weird people who have always been addressed by their first and last name (when you've got a last name like Fruits, people like to use it). I'm a mom of two beautiful children who drive me close to insanity, on the hour, every hour. I'm an average mom, and on some days below average. I've been a stay-at-home mom and a work-from-home mom, I've breastfed and formula fed. I've had the experience of having my partner home all the time, and then experienced what it felt like to have a partner gone for weeks on end. I tried to be hands-on and fun, and it turned out that for me, that involved my kids going to day care.

When my older child was born, I was having a hard time living up to my own standards for the mom I imagined I'd be. I don't know exactly what made me think I needed to be the perfect mom; probably every movie mom I've ever seen, or the fact that our parents' and grandparents' generations were all taught to be tight-lipped regarding the struggles of motherhood. I too was trying out for the "perfect mom" lead role. I wanted to be doing crafts and singing all day long, plus providing all organic everything, down to the pillowcases. I forgot to take into consideration how tired I was going to be, and how that would affect my giving a shit if what they ate was organic or not. When reality rolled around, I was happy if they ate *anything*.

The hardest adjustment of all was how alone I felt. While I was a stay-at-home mom, I was lost and stuck with my own thoughts, for hours and days on end. I was hurting my own feelings constantly. All I could think about were the things I was not and all the ways I wasn't measuring up. I'm writing the book I wish I'd had when I was crying by my bedside. Questioning every decision that led me up to this point. Wondering if I had ruined my life.

THE THING IS, THE DAY YOU MEET YOUR NEWBORN IS ALSO THE DAY YOU ARE MEETING THE NEW YOU.

I didn't realize that I would be relearning everything I thought I knew about the world around me simultaneously with my child. Becoming a mom broke all the rules I thought I'd live my life by—I dressed how I swore I would never dress, I gained and lost friendships, and I learned more about myself than I ever thought possible.

Motherhood has the potential to break you, but it also can mend you in ways you never expected.

Motherhood taught me how to stop "people pleasing." It taught me how to accept my imperfections and how to embrace the real me—someone I somehow had lost along the way before ever becoming a mom. As an overextended new mom, I no longer had the time or energy to waste on things that were unimportant to me or my family. It was in the two-hour nap-time window of freedom that I finally started asking, "What do I want?" Soon, I no longer strived for perfection and was pleased with achieving just "good enough." And after the dust settled from the explosion that is bringing humans into this life, I had shed not only the expectations of what it meant to be a mom, but also what it meant to be a woman.

Right up there with the realization that having a uterus should not make me the default house cleaner, I also realized my relationship with my husband was changing. Being in the trenches of raising little children didn't give me much time to myself, so when I did finally get a moment, I wanted to make the most of it—and that meant not doing anything I didn't want to do. This included, but was not limited to, *not* sleeping with my husband. After a couple months of self-reflection, discovery, and acceptance, I came out as a late-in-life lesbian. Everybody asked me, "How did you not know?"— which is a belittling question—but I'm thankful I had the courage to even look for the answer within myself. (And no, it wasn't the housecleaning that clued me in.)

I wrote this book while parenting a two-year-old and a four-year-old, living with my girlfriend and my husband, from whom I was romantically separated. I refer to them interchangeably throughout this book as "my partner." While the gender you're partnered with doesn't matter as much in the universal themes of parenthood, gender roles and expectations DO matter.

Neither of my partners is at fault for the male/female roles and expectations that were placed on them, but the assumptions—of who does what, and when—do suck. Men are not the only ones working these days. Women are expected to care for the kids as if they don't also work, and the sad truth is that men are just not held to the same standard.

Trying to be the perfect mother, wife, daughter, sister, friend means that we are doing a "good job" right? Maybe after we become "perfect" we will feel whole or enough, right? Wrong. We are not here to live our lives for others' stamp of approval. Our purpose and worth do not depend on perfection, but on living lives that are true to ourselves. In motherhood and everywhere else. There is no leaderboard. You already hold first place in the "you" category.

Motherhood is a metamorphosis, and while you may or may not experience the same exact changes I did, my goal is to shine the light on all the parental difficulties our parents' generation kept hush-hush, so you don't have to face them alone. That's what I want this book to be for you: a sigh of relief.

THIS IS NOT A PARENTING BOOK. INSTEAD OF TELLING YOU THE MOTHER YOU NEED TO BE, I'M HERE TO HELP YOU LOVE THE MOTHER YOU ALREADY ARE.

We were not meant to be perfect; it would teach our children nothing about the real world if we were. The world is not perfect, and neither are we.

We struggle with different parts of motherhood at different times, so choose your own adventure (aka chapters), whatever resonates for you. Please come back and reread what you need when you need it. My hope is that somewhere between these lines, you'll feel seen, validated, and secure, knowing you are not alone. Some of these chapters might make more sense at varying times, since motherhood is not linear, and we all experience different feelings at different times. I just ask that you listen and read with an open heart and open mind. I want to be here for you. Be the mom friend you've always needed, the one who shares too much, but who also makes you feel loved.

IT'S ALL NORMAL

As mothers, we are quick to assign ourselves the label of "failure" because we have unrealistic expectations of what motherhood is going to be.

We all need reminders on those hard days that motherhood is not all sunshine, cuddling, kids that do everything you ask the first time, and rainbows. It's more like shitstorms, tears, and the looming feeling that you're dying on the inside. It's all normal.

This is your safe space to admit motherhood sucks sometimes. That you love the shit out of your children, but don't feel the same about motherhood.

Each section of this book is a lesson I learned the hard way. I want to reassure you that you'll get through these chapters in your life, because moms and children are the most resilient creatures on this planet. We raise the future, one kiss good night at a time. Because of this, we also hold the keys to changing the future. Unlike the rest of the animal kingdom, whose children come out practically ready to hunt their own food, our children need our love and protection much longer. That's why it's hard. That's why we lose ourselves, we give so much until (sometimes) there's nothing left to give—because being a mom demands so much of our bodies, time, and minds. We become the stump that was once *The Giving Tree* (which is why *The Giving Tree* gives me hives, but I digress). Motherhood is a journey, not a destination. I have no shame saying that, some days, I wish it was a destination. One day the road will be less bumpy, your kids will be traveling off on their own paths, and you'll miss this crazy shit. (Or at least that's what I hear.)

YOU CAN LOVE THE SHIT OUT OF YOUR CHILDREN, BUT NOT FEEL THE SAME ABOUT MOTHERHOOD.

YOU HAVE TO FUCK UP

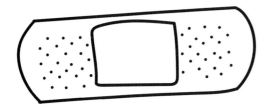

One day you'll forget a diaper and a change of clothes when you go to the park. And this will be the day that your baby will have a category five shit explosion up their back and into their hair. This will be the day you learn never to forget an extra pair of clothes and a diaper again. That's the beauty of motherhood: we are allowed to fuck up. Actually, we *have* to fuck up, that's how we learn.

Take this as permission to figure out what works and doesn't work for you and your family, without the guilt.

a mom when you understand how and why babies are cleaner than their parents

IT'S NOT CONSIDERED FAILING WHEN YOU'RE LEARNING.

I've heard about these mythical creatures: children that can be transferred from the car seat to their crib while continuing to nap. I've heard rumors of these magical babies who love broccoli at any time of the day. I've seen babies who hang out at weddings till midnight, yet I can't seem to get my child to stay up after 7 pm without losing his shit. I've prayed to have one of those kids who will eat anything you put in front of them. How will you know if you are one of the lucky chosen ones, if you don't try? That's why it's imperative that you push their limits (and yours) now and then.

You're supposed to "mess up." Messing up doesn't mean you've done something wrong. Seriously, how else will you learn!? It's not considered failing when you're learning. And because our children grow and change so quickly, our answers and discoveries will change as quickly as their shoe sizes.

You do not need a Pinterest-worthy home or nursery, you do not need to look like a pinup model, and you do not need to serve five-course meals with every color of the rainbow every night for dinner. You don't owe anyone perfection. We are human; fucking up is what we do best. Lean into it, Mama. I thought I was going to be this all-organic, wooden toys, no fast food, crafty kind of mom, but turns out I'm not. And I had a hard time accepting that I didn't live up to my own expectations.

Also, just a friendly reminder that the more effortless a mom makes motherhood look, the more effort she puts into making it look effortless. To be honest, that sounds completely exhausting. I'm already tired.

When I was a newbie mom on little to no sleep, I would never leave the house without under-eye concealer, even when I was going for a quick walk around the block with sunglasses on. I didn't want anyone to know I was having a hard time, or that my baby wasn't sleeping "through the night." I thought that meant I was doing something wrong and by default I thought I had to hide my pain. I also believed it meant I was a bad mom.

It's like so many other parts of being a woman we are told to hide—hide your period, hide your miscarriage, hide your struggles, hide anything that makes you harder to swallow. We don't have to water down ourselves to be more palatable to someone else. More on that later. Women are badass.

Mistakes are not a sign of weakness. They are a sign that we are trying and fighting.

It was harder for me to make mistakes with my first child because of that damn pressure to be the perfect mom that I had not unpacked yet. After putting him to sleep, I would not dare to go in the room. I was terrified of waking him up. Yes, I had a sound machine on full blast and the room completely blacked out. I feared waking him, thinking he would never go back to sleep. With my second, I will go in and squish his cheeks and even risk a photo if he's in an adorable sleeping position. You know they are the cutest when they are sleeping. I can't resist a sleeping baby.

ALSO, JUST A FRIENDLY REMINDER THAT THE MORE EFFORTLESS A MOM MAKES MOTHERHOOD LOOK, THE MORE EFFORT SHE PUTS INTO MAKING IT LOOK EFFORTLESS. TO BE HONEST, THAT SOUNDS COMPLETELY EXHAUSTING. I'M ALREADY TIRED.

What's the worst that can happen? He wakes up a little, I run out like a ninja on an obstacle course, and he goes back to sleep. The drive to sleep at night is strong—most nights he just readjusts and lets out not a peep.

We haven't had many opportunities to take both kids out to eat lately and to be frank, I was scared of the outcome. Taking two toddlers out to lunch, would I even get to eat? Then it happened: I couldn't convince my partner to order Uber Eats one more time and I needed a little outing myself, to be honest. Long story short, we survived. I ate, the kids threw shit on the floor, and they maybe consumed one French fry each. It wasn't awful, and we had some fun.

And now one example where **shit hit the fan.**

We took a flight. You already know where this is about to go. Our biggest fear as new mothers traveling with small children happened: my baby cried the whole flight. He wouldn't latch. He didn't want water. He didn't want a snack, and pacing the aisles didn't even help. Yet how I felt about it is what shocked me. I thought I was going to be sweating, worrying about all the other passengers. But in between the screams, I realized all I cared about was my baby. I didn't care about what anyone else thought. I knew in my heart that I was doing all I could. Isn't that all we can do in any given moment anyways?

You don't really know how a situation is going to make you feel until you go through it. Did I fuck up? Not technically, with this new set of rules I'm giving you as a mom. Did I feel this was a fuckup before I had kids? Definitely.

Shit is going to hit the fan sometimes. We will learn to never take a flight at naptime ever again…or that it wasn't so bad after all, and maybe it'll go better next time.

So go ahead: take the flight, try broccoli for the 100th time this month, let them nap in the car, go out to eat, risk it all for a photo while they are sleeping, do the things that you might have considered "fucking up" before children. It's all part of paving your own road through motherhood.

Disclaimer: I am not advocating taking safety risks. This is just to encourage you to bend your normal daily routines here and there if and when you feel up for it, mentally and emotionally.

you got this, Mama

LOVE CAN
Love can
TAKE TIME
take time

Believe it or not, it's normal to not instantly feel a connection with your new baby. Sometimes, the love can be instant and overwhelming; you'll feel like your heart is going to explode. For others, it takes time for that love to grow. **Both are normal.** As your connection grows, so will the love.

It's hard to love someone you have never met. With my first, I thought I was head over heels because the anticipation of the unknown was so exciting. In other words, I didn't know to be scared yet, **ha ha help.**

There's nothing like your first and nothing like your second.

My second pregnancy was different. I did not enjoy being 50 pounds heavier chasing a toddler, and I didn't have the time to romanticize this unknown baby in my belly. I didn't even know if it was possible for me to love another baby like I loved my first (a very common worry in moms before they have a second).

The love for my second grew after he was born. It was slow at first, because now that this wasn't my first rodeo, I wasn't in love with the "idea" of having a baby. I could focus more on loving him as an individual. Once that love hit—I will say it was after a couple months—it felt deeper than the first. Hold on, don't come at me with pitchforks.

I was a nervous first-time mom, and it made it hard for me to enjoy little moments. With my second, my love wasn't clouded by anxiety. My love for him was no bigger than for my first, it's just that I could *enjoy* the love more. I could actually enjoy him being little and needing to be held all the time, because I knew it wasn't going to be this way forever. With the first child you think these challenging moments are here to stay. With the second, I spend less time worrying about milestones and more time staring into his wide eyes. I know now that he will need me a little less every day. That is the most beautiful and heartbreaking part of motherhood.

There's nothing like your first and nothing like your second. Having a second child is like riding a bike: you know how to make it go. It doesn't make the ride any less tiring, you just know how to keep upright without falling too frequently.

They say you can't pick favorites either, but…I'm just kidding. I love my sons deeply for different reasons. My older one is calm and careful, smart and independent, and I love those things about him. My second is crazy, but that means crazy fun, crazy intense, and crazy affectionate. Your children will fill up your heart in different ways than mine.

I do pick favorites for the day, and it's usually the one who stayed in their bed the night before. It's like having an employee of the day: they will still get paid with love and kisses, but just one of them will get their picture on the wall with no extra compensation.

If you are reading this, and you've got a tiny human in your arms and are wondering *What the fuck did I just do?* don't worry, you are not alone. I remember sitting in my rocking chair nursing my son for the 100th time by 6:00 am, wondering why do people even have children? This shit is hard! **I talked myself off the ledge by saying that people willingly have more than one child, so it has to get better…and it did, and it will.**

Some people love the newborn stage and will have no clue what I'm even talking about. Some moms love having toddlers, or middle-school-aged kids, or teens (though I've never heard of one). You'll find your jam. Every season of motherhood isn't for everyone.

It can be very triggering to hear how someone loves, say, newborns when you really struggled with that phase. It can feel like something is wrong with us if we don't love every season of motherhood.

NO ONE CAN TELL YOU WHICH PHASE OF MOTHERHOOD IS THE HARDEST, BECAUSE USUALLY IT FEELS LIKE THE ONE YOU ARE LIVING THROUGH RIGHT NOW IS THE HARDEST.

Your love for your children and love for motherhood will change and evolve, just as you and your kids will, too.

YOU ARE NOT REQUIRED TO BOUNCE BACK

You just had a baby, and you don't recognize the woman in the mirror. Who is she?

Dark circles, stained clothes, and hair that's definitely surpassed the socially acceptable number of dry shampooings. Is this even your body? Were you switched at birth? You waited nine months to push out this baby and reclaim this body for your own, but why does it feel like you're still living in a stranger's house? You're uncomfortable, lost, and almost always tired.

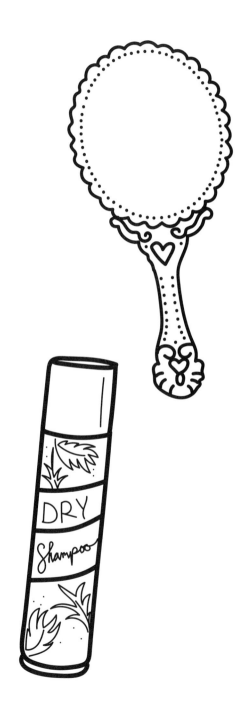

MISSING

Spontaneous
loved 2 travel
well rested
clean hair
could finish thoughts

The breasts that were once full and youthful flop out from your top every time you bend over. Your body is softer than ever before, with some extra lines in its story. Oh, and you can't decide which is worse, the hair loss that has you questioning if you are part German shepherd, or the postpartum regrowth where—with just the right amount of hairspray—you could dress up as a lion this Halloween or any day of the week.

It can be hard witnessing our bodies shift, change, and age right before our very own eyes. Here's the thing: if we were meant to stay young forever, we would.

This new body of yours needs the same if not more love than your old body; it still houses you and that will never change. Your body needs time and space to heal, and you need time and space to grow into your new role. This doesn't mean you can't eat healthy and work out if you want to, but do not punish your new body, and more important, do not punish yourself. You both just went through one of the hardest transitions in life.

WORTHY

Please don't focus on the numbers on the scale or deprive yourself of food when you are hungry. You too need nourishment and the things that will make you feel supported through these sometimes seemingly endless, monotonous days. You deserve to treat yourself when you can.

DON'T TRY TO CUT OUT THINGS THAT SPARK JOY FOR YOU.

THIS

PLEASE READ THAT AGAIN. YOU DESERVE JOY, YOU NEED IT.

We are conditioned to think that we have to bounce back after having a baby. This may come from a place deep inside of us where we miss our old life, but it's also where the media jumps right in to tell us, "You are not enough. Buy these things to make yourself feel better. Buy this idea that you need to be a size 0, and look at all these other women who *bounced back* and compare yourself to them." We cannot and should not compare ourselves to these models who fit into their size 0 jeans two seconds after giving birth. Why not, you might ask? Because (in most cases) we were not a size 0 before we got pregnant.

If they really did slip back into their size 0 pants, ask yourself why. If they are a model, then it truly is their job to get their pre-baby body back. That's how they make a living; or maybe they really enjoy working out. Instead of comparing our bodies to those of other moms, we have to remember that their story is not the same as ours. Maybe she has more support than you, more time to herself, maybe that is how she takes her "me time." Or maybe she has a super-fast metabolism. **Genetics can be assholes sometimes.**

IT'S IMPORTANT TO REMEMBER THAT THE SIZE OF YOUR WAIST DOES NOT DETERMINE YOUR WORTH.

We do not have to be perfect to be considered beautiful. Women have been conditioned to think that our worth is only defined by how our bodies look. Yet that's the least interesting thing about us, and what we do with our bodies means so much more. Our bodies are all capable of doing amazing and vastly different things, and that, my friend, is what makes us all beautiful.

I love social media, except for when I'm cursing it, but sometimes it has a way of showing us everything we are not. This is your sign to unfollow anyone who makes you feel bad about yourself. We are on a different mission from here on out. Besides, 99.9 percent of what we see on social media is probably fake anyways. That saying "If it's too good to be true, it probably is" applies here especially. Slowly we are seeing more variety online about what makes a beautiful body, and the more exposure the better. The more we see, the more we'll know that we are not alone and not the minority.

Culturally there is a shift happening. Day by day we are normalizing average-sized bodies, and not only will this help boost our own confidence, it will also teach our children to love their own bodies. I grew up in the era where bodies of various shapes and sizes were considered plus size. Don't you want the narrative to be different for your children? Society plays a major role in mirroring our insecurities, but we can start the change at home, with ourselves.

Repeat after me: My body is beautiful. My body is home. My body holds otherworldly magical comfort to the ones I love and those who love me. My imperfections are now to be identified as perfections, because there is nothing imperfect about them. They are what makes me me.

It's normal to think about your pre-baby body and mourn where your boobs used to live. Which feels like the penthouse suite compared to where they are now, but they—and you— have not decreased in value. If anything, the experience your boobs have acquired now makes them overly qualified, seasoned, and wise. Actually, they are now retired. They've moved south where it's warmer, and they can relax for once in their lives. They finished their tit Olympics and won breast in show. They've been through a lot, let's thank them for their hard work. Let them be. Let them exist. And the same thing goes for you.

LISTEN, MAMA, THIS BODY OF YOURS IS A BODY OF HONOR.

All the blood, sweat, and tears that have poured out of you to bring life into this world is remarkable. Fucking remarkable. Remember that the next time that voice in your head tries to tell you otherwise.

Your body means home to these little humans, they love it just the way it is, and they are always watching. The way we talk to ourselves will be the way they speak to themselves. The more you love your body, the more your partner will, too. They say confidence is sexy, and they are not wrong.

Other people's opinions of our bodies are none of our business. How we speak to ourselves means more. If your partner is unloving and unforgiving of your new body, that says more about them than it does about you. Maybe they are projecting their own insecurities and conditioned expectations of what it means to be a woman, mother, and wife. You do not need to fit into an outdated mold of what it means to be beautiful.

I want you to get comfortable with the idea that you don't owe anyone perfection:

not yourself, not your partner, and especially not your children (but more on that in a later chapter). This is just the new narrative for your physical body. It's liberating a little, don't you think? To be allowed to be yourself, to not be confined to anyone's beauty standards but your own? Because isn't that what makes us each marvelous in our own way? We all are allowed to blossom as different types of flowers, each charming and exquisite and unique.

OWN IT, MAMA.

The tired eyes, the saggy skin, the stretch marks, the seasoned boobs, everything. All of it.

The truth is, this is your new body. Maybe you don't love it now, but let's try to appreciate what it has done for us and maybe over time you'll learn to love it a little more each day.

I DO...
NOT
REMEMBER
HATING MY
PARTNER

CAN YO

I've heard from previous generations this advice for a happy marriage: to put your partner first, even after having kids, and honestly—WTF? I just pushed a baby out of my vagina, and now I'm supposed to not only cater to this really needy new human I just made, but also my partner? Does your partner need to be fed and burped and diaper-changed every 2 to 3 hours? No. So this advice is as outdated as it is ludicrous. Plus, when was the last time a male partner got told to put his wife's needs first? The uncharted territory of parenthood is not claimed for moms and moms only, it's *your* new journey together.

I love how women are expected to meet everyone else's needs before their own. What in the fucking '50s housewife is this kind of ass-backward bullshit?

This is why so many new moms feel undersupported. They are told to put their marriage and baby first, which pretty much means to put aside their own needs so that everyone else is happy. Often this translates into: have sex with your partner when you don't feel like it. Put the baby first and forget your own needs and wants, or you're a bad mom.

Let me just clear one thing up for everyone. Having a child is hard on a marriage. It doesn't make your marriage any less because of it. It's just normal. It doesn't mean your marriage is doomed.

Did I feel like I hated my partner those first couple of weeks and/or months? Yes. Was I feeling frustrated that my needs were going unmet, lost in my new role, and completely out of control of my own life? Also, yes. I remember feeling like everything was off. We couldn't communicate, we couldn't relax, we could hardly have fun together, we were miserable.

It's easy to take out our anger on those closest to us. Ask yourself, why do you feel angry? Is it because their life seemingly went unchanged, and yours was completely flipped upside down and put back together backwards, and you resent them a little for it? Too specific? Well, that was me. I saw him going to work and all I could feel was jealousy. After some deep diving of my own, I realized I didn't want him to not leave, I just wanted to be able to walk out of the house without the weight and worry of being a mom sometimes. I wanted to be able to sit down and eat a hot meal someone else had prepared. I wanted to talk to other adults and feel like a person again. Feeling these things doesn't make you a bad mom, it makes you human. Just because you had a baby doesn't mean you don't have any needs of your own!

I'll admit, I thought it was less than romantic to tell my partner exactly what I wanted and needed all day long, but I realized that if I was having a hard time knowing what I needed and wanted, how could I expect someone else to read my mind? After weeks of internalizing and wondering why we hadn't instantly become the perfect parents we assumed we'd be before we had kids, I knew something had to give; and it was my expectations of what I thought my marriage and partnership was supposed to look like after kids.

BEING THE DEFAULT PARENT COMES WITH MANY BLESSINGS AND *SOME* CURSES.

If you are the default parent, the kids want you, and no one else will do: when they are sick, to tuck them in bed at night, to make their waffles just the way they like, to find their missing shoes, or to wash their hair in the way only we know how. While this is sometimes—okay, mostly always—exhausting, yes, being the default parent holds a special kind of hidden magic, too.

We know what our kids want and need when they need it. That doesn't mean we can't delegate other tasks in the house, or outside of the home.

Adjusting our expectations will help us appreciate what we do have, versus what we don't. Moms (historically speaking) are great multitaskers, schedule organizers, mental grocery list keepers, and built-in calendars, just to name a few. Okay, we are badass, I'll just say it. And some partners may do a great job of taking over these tasks naturally. If you have one of these unicorn partners, maybe you should play the lottery? Though it seems you already won. As for the rest of us, we have to guide our partners on how to be helpful, and there is no shame in that (though yes, it is annoying).

This is where the C word comes in. No, not that one. The other C word: *communication.* I know, I know, it's so cliché. Hear me out: our partners are not acting in some new, hot, romantic comedy. They will not say the perfectly scripted one-liners that will make you giggle-snort and forget you were ever mad in the first place. They are tired, confused, and feeling drained, too.

When my partner and I used to attend dinner parties, I inevitably found myself alone chasing our kid in some unbabyproofed new location; and I would never get a chance

to look up and enjoy conversation with other adults. If you had asked me in this moment if I hated my partner, I would have said yes. Now when we go to family functions, we play *"Tag, you're it!"* A verbal confirmation reminds the other to take over; it is easy to get caught up in conversation and not want to chase after little kids, but we both decided to have them, so we both are going to take turns watching them. Caring for humans is not just a woman's job. I realized that my partner needs guidance sometimes, because what I want isn't always obvious. Was it frustrating? Yes, but would I rather guide someone who is in my life so we operate better as a team rather than just wait for them to figure it out on their own, which might be never? Also yes.

Delegate who does what and when, like the organizational genius you are, Mama. I use the same trick on my toddler that I do on my partner. I ask, "Do you want to give the kids a bath, or clean up the kitchen?" and for my toddler it's "Do you want to read a book, or watch five more minutes of YouTube before bed?" I give them two options; it conveys a sense of urgency while implying that they get to choose. It doesn't have a 100 percent success rate, but it does mean I don't have to do everything for everyone in the house, and *that* is the goal.

Divide and conquer, so you don't have to do it all. Maybe your idea of cleanliness isn't the same, or the dead plants in your front yard are not as much of an eyesore to your partner as they are to you. The only way to know is to talk about it.

It's important to make sure both of you are getting what you need. If your partner takes the whole Saturday doing things they enjoy, don't feel guilty asking for a day the following weekend for you. You deserve a day (or a year, but let's be realistic here), and they should watch the kids so you can feel human, too.

Something else to consider: if your partner can't give you what you need, it doesn't mean they are the only person available to help. If you can afford it, hire someone to help you. If the mother-in-law is begging to help, let her. If a friend offers to help, accept it. We can't all be great at everything.

Identify feelings of resentment before they harden into hate. You'll probably uncover a different reason as to why you feel this way.

We may think we hate our partners, but we don't actually hate them. We're just tired and need more support.

WE MAY THINK WE HATE OUR PARTNERS, BUT WE DON'T ACTUALLY HATE THEM. WE'RE JUST TIRED AND NEED MORE SUPPORT.

IT'S OKAY TO HAVE ZERO SEXUAL APPETITE

After I had my kids, I lost all interest in sex. Any mom I felt comfortable enough talking about this with said they felt the same. This is probably why it took me a while to figure out my sexuality; the issue is so common, it was years before I began to question whether my particular situation meant something else. Thousands of jokes, videos, and conversations later, the takeaway remains the same: most new moms don't want to have sex with their partner.

How does one give themselves all day long to a tiny, very needy human and be expected to just rip off our clothes and be thrilled with

MY LOVE LANGUAGE AFTER KIDS: DON'T TOUCH ME, DON'T TALK TO ME.

excitement to give ourselves *yet one more time*? How can we expect this when we are completely exhausted and "touched out"?

Spoiler alert: We can't.

When I was a new mom, I hardly had enough time to take care of myself. Some days I couldn't even manage a shower, let alone handle another

person under this roof needing and wanting more from me. After a long day of unconditional motherly love, I didn't want anyone or anything touching me.

If you feel the same way, you are not alone.

80 PERCENT OF WOMEN AGREE THEY TOO LOST THEIR SEX DRIVE AFTER KIDS. 80 FUCKING PERCENT, AND NO ONE IS TALKING ABOUT THIS?

Of course, we don't talk about it. We think there is something wrong with us or with our relationship. Hear me now on this: It does not matter whether you are deeply in love or you are not—I have been both while parenting young children, and the fact remains that some nights you are just too touched out to have the bandwidth for physical intimacy.

With my first child, I had a third-degree tear and bled for eight weeks straight. It was a little traumatic, to say the least. I did not want anything in or around my vagina and as a result, we did not have sex for six deeply shame-drenched months. Even then, the only reason we did was because I felt guilt. My partner didn't make me feel guilty, I put it all on myself.

The media tells us that if we're not pulsing with desire at all times, we're sad and wrong and past our prime. As women, we are so quick to blame ourselves, even though losing sex drive after birth is actually normal. In fact, the vagina doesn't even produce lubricant while a woman is breastfeeding! The more I began to open up about this issue with other women, the more they felt comfortable confiding in me that they felt the same way, too.

Here's something helpful that I learned: There are two kinds of sexual desire, responsive and spontaneous.

Spontaneous is the gush and rush of emotions you see portrayed in the movies. Like, yeah, I want some of whatever they are having. This is common in the beginning of your relationships, and it's normal for it to fade away.

The second kind is *responsive,* when a person doesn't feel turned on until they start engaging in sexual activity. Then their desire level responds to the physical acts. Many people, especially women, experience desire this way.

Although you can experience both at different times and with different people, the point is that they are both normal and healthy ways of thinking about sexual desire. If you fall into the responsive category, figure out what you do *respond* to, and only if you want to. Because when you're a mom, you will have nights when you feel completely touched out, you're exhausted, or you just need some time to yourself. You can have all the tricks and tools to turn your night into a masterpiece, but if you are too tired, you will be responsive to nothing. Knowing that is powerful; getting to know your own body is powerful.

THERE ARE TWO KINDS OF SEXUAL DESIRE,

I would have given my right tit for this information 3.5 years ago and my right tit was the producing tit, if you know what I mean. I thought that because I never had the spontaneous sexual desire, there was something wrong with me.

SCREAMING INTERNALLY THROUGH MY VAGINA

As if aligning arousal and sexual relationships with your partner after having kids wasn't already hard enough, let's talk about the orgasm gap.

90 percent of men experience orgasms during intercourse, compared to 50 percent of women.

WHAT THE ACTUAL FUCK?

No wonder we are never in the mood. There's a fifty-fifty chance we are not going to finish. Why get ourselves all riled up and then have to roll over and go to sleep after we are left with the lights on?

Bottom line is, sex after kids is different because we are different. We have less energy, less time to ourselves to recharge, and less time, period, because we need sleep. Sexy time is another opportunity for us to learn about ourselves, since time and energy are limited (thanks, kids). We need to figure out what we really like and need in the bedroom so we get the most BANG for our buck. (Ha ha—see what I did there?) Maybe introduce some female-focused toys into the bedroom—and by female-focused toys, I mean clitoral stimulation toys, because they are amazing—I know firsthand. Moral of my sexual story is that we can say no, married or not. We can prioritize our needs and wants. It's not unladylike. Giving and giving with no return will burn us out even quicker than we realize. Understanding that I am in charge of my own pleasure has been powerful and also puts less pressure on my partner. That if we can't get there together, I won't worry, I can do it on my own…and if anyone feels insecure about that, they have their own soul searching to do.

FED IS BEST, STILL

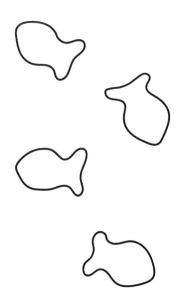

This statement will never go out of style. It holds true from the minute your baby leaves your uterus until the day they move out of your home, when you finally no longer have to answer the looming question of "What the fuck am I going to cook them for dinner?" every night.

Feed your baby, no matter what age, the way that works best for you. We have enough pressure on us as mothers. If breastfeeding doesn't work for you? Stop. It is no longer liquid gold if it costs you your sanity. I don't give a shit what these sanctimonious moms say on Facebook. Bottle or breast is no longer a debate; feed your baby the

OUR CHILDREN DON'T CARE HOW WE FEED THEM, THEY JUST WANT TO BE FED.

way that best works for you and your family. You are no more or less of a mother for either outcome. We think because breastfeeding is "natural," it's supposed to come naturally. That is not the case for everyone.

For the moms who are unable to produce enough, I'm proud of you for moving on and putting your babies' needs first. For the moms who are able to produce enough, I'm proud of you for sacrificing your body to do so. As a society, we can be proud of both. See how easy that was?

I breastfed my first child for a year—but wait, there's more. At three months, a lump appeared in my breast. At first, it was the size of a pea, but it soon turned into a lemon. My doctor kept telling me it was just a clogged duct and to work it out in the hot shower. I scraped, I massaged, I had my husband suck, and I used a wooden kitchen spoon to try to get this clogged duct out. After days of torture and sunflower lecithin pills, I just knew: I needed an ultrasound. Come to find out, my lemon was a breast abscess that needed to be drained. Yes, a needle was stuck into my boob, while I was awake. Yet even after this, I kept breastfeeding, knowing there was a chance that my little lovely lemon lump might return.

I didn't continue breastfeeding because I loved it, I continued because I was scared to stop. I thought that to be a great mom, I needed to breastfeed for a year—emphasis on *need.* I was scared to stop because I'd been told my child would get sick, that he would not grow, and what if he didn't like formula? I felt I couldn't do anything that might hinder his growth toward becoming the best little human he could be.

I wanted to quit breastfeeding when my child was six months old. I just couldn't seem to get him to take the bottle, and I was tired of trying. I got really lucky, and he weaned himself by his first birthday. That was a weird feeling, almost like being rejected, since it was his choice before it was mine. We can never win, ha ha ha—help!

My second breastfeeding experience came to a halt around six months, the moment I realized I was just tired of whipping out my boobs every couple hours, worried about how much he was getting all day and night, worried about if I accidentally had dairy (he had a dairy intolerance). It was all just too much for me. This was 2020, and we were stuck inside: logistically, it couldn't have been a better recipe for me to continue breastfeeding. But I was over it. I felt a bit of shame, but realized I couldn't be the only one to openly admit I no longer wanted to breastfeed. I stopped.

Just because you can keep going doesn't mean you *have* to.

As mothers, we give so much to our children. Cleaning, wiping, cooking, snacking, playing, singing, loving, hugging. Feeding them from your breast or from the bottle does not make or break your worth as a mother. Look at everything else you do for them.

Some moms just love breastfeeding, and this chapter will not make any sense to them. If this is you, I am also happy for you; this is mainly for the moms who are struggling with breastfeeding, to relieve yet another guilt-evoking part of motherhood.

Our children don't care how we feed them, they just want to be fed. And a happy mom almost always equals a happy baby. Okay yes, you can get some pushback during the switching process from boob to bottle, but we generally are the ones who make the biggest deal about the breast or bottle debate. The littles are just crying because they are hungry and don't like change. You both will get through it. One day at a time, or one feed at a time, like the rest of the infancy shitshow.

I understand it's easy to wear the guilt of wanting to breastfeed but not being able to, and I wish I could also take away this pain for you. Tell yourself you did the best you could and that you are no less of a mother because you could not breastfeed. We all struggle in motherhood in different ways, and this is just part of your story, your journey. You are enough. You did your best. Now stop beating yourself up about it, please and thank you.

I wanted to stop breastfeeding because I wanted my body back. We are allowed to still want and need things for ourselves after becoming mothers. I remember the feeling from when my first weaned, how my body became my own again. I didn't realize how much I needed this until it happened. I felt liberated knowing there would be no more leaking, letdowns, or wearing only the clothes in which I could feed at a moment's notice.

Formula babies are happy and healthy babies, just like the ones who drink breast milk. And it's not like breastfed babies never want to eat a chicken nugget off the car floor. If you are stressed from breastfeeding, then that makes you and your baby stressed. You must do what works for you, and that will look different to every family.

Beyond the boob, I also didn't turn out to be the baking-muffins-with-hidden-vegetables kind of mom I thought I was going to be. There are more picky eaters than not, so do the best you can, nothing more. Even pressuring them into eating things they don't want to eat makes it worse, so just feed your children what works. Sure, offer them broccoli when you eat it, but in all seriousness, how often do you want to eat broccoli? Do you want fruits and vegetables at every meal? So maybe it's the same for your little humans, too.

My first son lived off corn dogs and peanut butter and jelly sandwiches for almost a whole year. My second lives off cheese and bread and will occasionally try our foods; and I think that's because we put less pressure on him to try them.

We are all doing the best we can, and that's the best we can do. We eat what we want, when we want it. Why would we hold our littles to different standards?

Fed is still best, Mama. There is no reason for you to feel guilty feeding your children the things they like to eat. They will go through phases, like only eating buttered noodles (I go through that phase, too, sometimes). The kids are going to be okay. Throw in some gummy vitamins and just remember you are doing the best you can. Our best will look different on different days, and the same holds true for our children.
I get in feeding-little-humans ruts, on the daily. For more tips on feeding your kids various foods and how, you can follow Jenny from **@solidstarts** on Instagram. She has made it her life's mission to normalize feeding our children solid foods.

WTF ARE FPA AND FPD?

I didn't know that postpartum anxiety was a condition until after I had my second child. Someone asked me on Instagram if I had PPD or PPA with my first, and though I knew PPD stood for postpartum depression, I'd never heard of PPA.

Postpartum anxiety is when a person experiences excessive anxiety during the postpartum period, which is the period following childbirth. It can become so severe that it may interfere with a person's ability to function in everyday tasks.

SYMPTOMS

Though postpartum anxiety and postpartum depression are not the same, some estimates claim between 25 and 50 percent of people with anxiety disorders also develop postpartum depression in the two months following childbirth.

Everyone experiences anxiety differently. But people with postpartum anxiety experience thoughts that are usually:

- uncontrollable
- racing
- consuming
- disrupting
- overwhelming
- recurrent
- irrational (not logical or realistic)
- frightening

These uncontrollable, consuming thoughts tend to center on a few major areas of worry, such as:

- fears about the baby's and one's own health
- fears about a parent or partner becoming ill or dying
- a sense that something bad will happen
- irrational obsessions or fears
- blaming oneself excessively when something goes wrong
- feeling excessively guilty

Postpartum anxiety can also cause physical symptoms, including:

- unexplained exhaustion
- trouble sleeping
- trouble concentrating
- increased irritability
- muscle tension
- feeling on edge, restless, or wound up
- a rapid heartbeat
- feeling panicky for no clear reason

(Source: Medical News Today, "What to Know about Postpartum Anxiety," 2022.)

Postpartum depression may be mistaken for baby blues at first—but the signs and symptoms are more intense and last longer, and may eventually interfere with your ability to care for your baby and handle other daily tasks. Symptoms usually develop within the first few weeks after giving birth, but may begin earlier—during pregnancy—or later—up to a year after birth.

Postpartum depression signs and symptoms may include:

- Depressed mood or severe mood swings
- Excessive crying
- Difficulty bonding with your baby
- Withdrawing from family and friends
- Loss of appetite or eating much more than usual
- Inability to sleep (insomnia) or sleeping too much
- Overwhelming fatigue or loss of energy
- Reduced interest and pleasure in activities you used to enjoy
- Intense irritability and anger
- Fear that you're not a good mother
- Hopelessness
- Feelings of worthlessness, shame, guilt, or inadequacy
- Diminished ability to think clearly, concentrate, or make decisions
- Restlessness
- Severe anxiety and panic attacks
- Thoughts of harming yourself or your baby
- Recurrent thoughts of death or suicide
- Untreated, postpartum depression may last for many months or longer.

(Source: Mayo Clinic, "Postpartum Depression—Symptoms and Causes," 2022.)

IT WOULD BE BETTER TO
SEEK HELP, AND LATER
REALIZE YOU DIDN'T
REALLY NEED IT, THAN
TO LIVE MONTHS WITH
ANXIETY OR DEPRESSION
THAT YOU DIDN'T NEED
TO SUFFER THROUGH.

And after figuring out what PPA stood for I felt like I had been slapped across the face. **I had PPA? PPA IS A THING? WHY DID I NOT KNOW THIS SOONER!?**

If you didn't know about PPA, now you do, and you can get help. Having PPA was hard on my marriage, my capacity for fun, and my overall ability to function. It made every part of my day difficult. It felt like I was running late to a very important date, all day, every day. Keeping my child on a schedule was the only way I felt like I had any control over my days, and if we were one minute late, and he took any length of time falling asleep, I blamed myself.

I remember hearing once upon a time that I'd be able to tell the difference between sleepy cries and hunger cries when I had a baby, because they sound distinct. For me, all the cries sounded the same, because I was too nervous to tell the difference. I lived in a constant state of fight or flight. My son had to eat dinner at 6 pm on the dot or I was convinced he would not sleep all night. I would lose sleep anticipating him not sleeping (even when he always slept). It was debilitating and exhausting.

Everyday situations felt like life or death. I couldn't leave my son with anyone, for fear he would die. I was suffocating myself in my own thoughts. It felt like everyone was just too lax with their rules and attention, because I was so hypervigilant. I would watch my husband at social gatherings take his eyes off the kids for one second, and it would send me spiraling.

Unfortunately, these warning signs sound a lot like what most moms experience those first few weeks of motherhood, and that's probably why some of us don't get help when we should.

If you are questioning whether this is you, my advice would be to seek help. Ask a professional. There are self-assessments online and many options for therapy: video, messaging, or in person. It wouldn't be the end of the world if you signed up for something you maybe didn't need as much as you thought you did. The *better safe than sorry* adage applies here. It would be better to seek help, and later realize you didn't really need it, than to live months with anxiety or depression that you didn't need to suffer through.

AS MOMS, WE SUFFER THROUGH SO MUCH THAT SOMETIMES WE FORGET WE DON'T HAVE TO ENDURE EVERYTHING.

I had crippling anxiety with my first child, and it never seemed to go away until I had a second. Now, I'm not advocating for you to have more children, I'm pointing this out to say that just because you experience anxiety with one child doesn't mean you will with subsequent babies.

The day my two boys were supposed to meet was a day I began to dream about ever since I found out I was pregnant with my younger child. And when I say dreamed, I mean made up fears, too. How they would hate each other, how I would regret bringing home another child, and how my first would never forgive me or love me again. I'm putting this into writing for anyone wondering if their thoughts are normal. Don't worry, they are.

I was so anxious waiting for my husband to pick us up from the hospital, I almost had a panic attack. And you know what? None of those things I was worrying about happened. My sons don't hate each other; they don't hate me; and I couldn't imagine my life without the two of them.

My anxiety likes to lie to me and help me come up with racing thoughts I cannot control. After two anxiety-free years, I've recently started feeling like anxiety wants to take up residence in my body again, and so I signed myself up for therapy right away. I'm not going to suffer through this a second time without help, and you shouldn't either.

MOTHERHOOD CAN BE TRAUMATIC.

There's no shame in saying that. Our lives are flipped upside down, and we are left to navigate these new journeys, sometimes with little to no help. But it doesn't have to be that way. Just because our parents "did it alone," or grandparents like to remind us how little they truly had, doesn't mean *you* have to suffer through it, too. It doesn't make you more of a mother for not needing help, and it doesn't make you any less of a mother for needing help.

I feel like every mom needs therapy at some point or another when going through this life-changing transition. Sometimes, this is where mom friends step in and can help you get through some of the cloudy days. If it's not enough just to vent, and if you find yourself emotionally dumping too much on others, it's time for a professional.

Also, if talk therapy is not enough and you need to take medicine, that doesn't make you a bad mother. Acknowledging that you need help and acting on it makes you a badass mom, not a bad one.

JUST BECAUSE YOU CAN DO IT ALONE DOESN'T MEAN YOU HAVE TO. THERE'S NO AWARD FOR BEING THE MOST STRESSED-OUT MOM.

For more information, see:

"What to know about postpartum anxiety." 2022. Medicalnewstoday.com. https://www.medicalnewstoday.com/articles/postpartum-anxiety.

"Postpartum Depression—Symptoms and Causes." 2022. Mayo Clinic. https://www.mayoclinic.org/diseases-conditions/postpartum-depression/symptoms-causes/syc-20376617.

I DIDN'T ASK, SO DON'T TELL

are ? ?

? . . A

?

?

is
he
sleeping

the nigh

?

How many times has someone given you unsolicited parenting advice, and not only was it not helpful (for so many reasons), but it was also a little hurtful? When you're caught off guard, or on little sleep, uncalled-for comments can make you question yourself, or, at the very least, just piss you off.

Maybe it was a family member telling you how your child *should* be sleeping by now, or a friend telling you how to feed your baby, or a complete stranger asking you

95

if you're going to have another baby. When did everybody become an expert on *your* parenting?

HERE'S THE THING: THE ADVICE ISN'T FOR YOU.

IT'S FOR THEM.

It's what worked for them once upon a time, and it literally has nothing to do with you and your baby. It's a form of nostalgia…for them.

You know how good it feels when you can guess what your baby needs and wants and everything in the world feels right again? That's what they are regifting to themselves but directing toward you. They are taking a trip down memory lane, and you're just in the passenger seat. You're an innocent bystander on the sidewalk, about to get hit because they can't stay in their own lane.

Their comments are to their past selves and that's also why they feel so entitled, or sure it will work, because it worked for them. We all know different things work for different children, and really, we just guess and check until something clicks. That's motherhood.

Take these unsolicited parenting tips and comments with a grain of salt. If these commenters have kids, they are just reliving their parenting. If they don't…well, then they can shove that advice up their asses. They know nothing. I don't care how much they love their fur-baby.

As for the nosy neighbor or lady at the mall asking when are you going to have more kids, or if you're going to try for a girl, or any other intrusive question? They are trying to relate and make conversation (or they just like the sound of their own voices). They don't mean it like we take it—I know, because I've been there, too. They think they are asking a harmless question, without taking into consideration what it took to have the children they see before them.

You know how with the age-old question "How are you doing?" you're supposed to answer with "Fine, thank you" instead of how you really feel? Feel free to use fake answers for these questions:

- When are you getting married?
- When are you starting a family?
- When are you going to have another?
- Are you going to try for a boy/girl?
- When are you going to **SHUT THE FUCK UP**—whoa, sorry, lost myself there for a second.

I can come up with a ton of reasons why people ask these dumb questions, but it all boils down to them experiencing nostalgia and simply not knowing what else to say/ask.

That's why we can't take it personally. Because it's not about us.

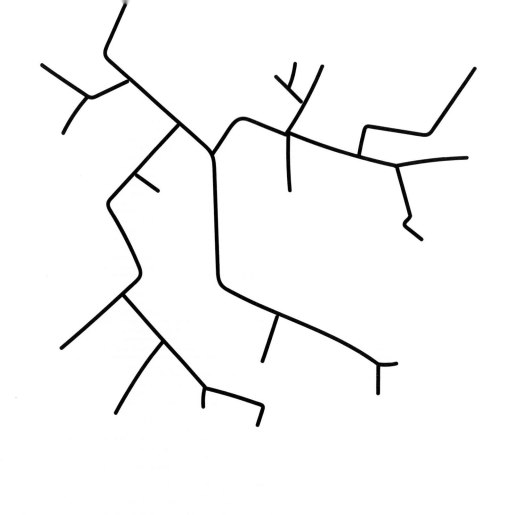

IF IT AIN'T BROKEN... UM, BREAK IT

I swore to **never** let my kids sleep in my room.

I swore they would **never** eat processed or fast food.

I swore my house would **never** overflow with rainbow plastic toys.

I swore my kids would **never** have their own iPads.

What idiot made up these rules?!
Oh yeah, it was me.

These are the rules I created for my family before I had a family. When I broke them, I felt worse than if I had robbed a bank. I forgot that I was the

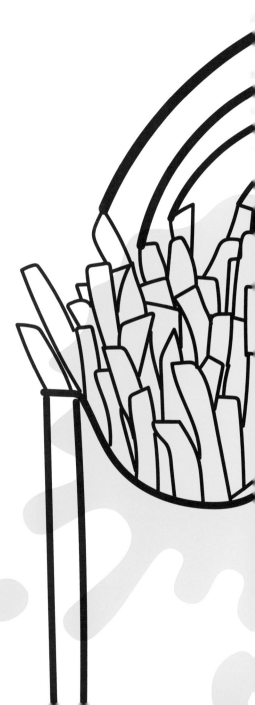

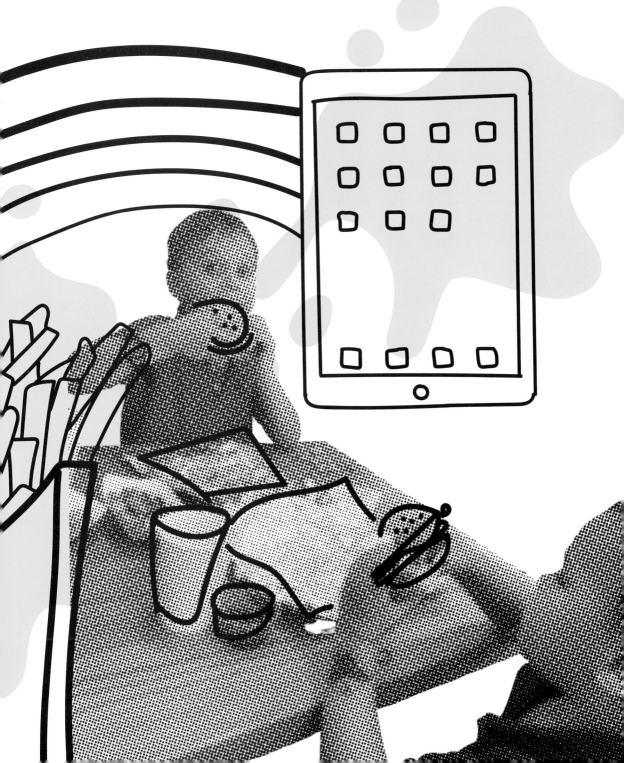

one who had created them, so I was allowed to break them. Besides, I made them before I had even met my children.

Breaking our own rules is something that will happen from time to time, if not every day. The way we perceive our actions, though, is the difference between a rise in cortisol and stress, or acceptance and love. We don't need ANY extra stress, so let's work on that acceptance and love part.

From time to time, I would let my son sleep in between my partner and me. I would stay up questioning myself all night, filled with guilt well into the next day. Overtired and now stressed. Great combo.

Then I realized the truth: I'm just breaking *my own* rules. No one is going to take my children from me because I let them fall asleep in my bed. In all seriousness, what was I afraid of? I was trying so hard to live up to standards I created before I knew shit about shit. That woman meant well, but would I take advice from her now? Nope.

As I mentioned earlier, I felt I needed to be the perfect mother even before I ever spent a millisecond actually being one. I think over time, women collect small ideas about what is expected of mothers—from movies, books, and social media, from friends and family members—and all these ideas stack up into a paragon of perfection, a mother who has all the answers, never tires, and always puts others' needs above her own.

Here's an example—in a film I recently watched, I noticed a generic scene with a mom cooking dinner. It was pitch black outside (as parents, we know this often means it's far past bedtime), yet in this fantasy, the daughter was not having a tantrum from exhaustion, but quietly sitting at the table doing a *painting* project. FWIW, she looked like she was two years old. She was also dressed like she was ready for a babyGap photo shoot. No need for supervision; she was just quietly entertaining her clean little self while her mom cooked.

This wasn't the plot of the movie, just a passing scene, but as a mom, I thought to myself that would never fucking happen in my house. It's the perfect example of how motherhood is deceptively portrayed in movies—calm, organized, manageable. Before you have children of your own, it's easy to believe that this could be an accurate representation. These fairy-tale images are spoon-fed quietly into everyone's subconscious, where they are compiled into secret notes of what motherhood is "supposed" to look like. Spoiler alert: that ain't it—but you already know that.

I thought giving up everything for my children was the only way to be a mother, because my grandma did that, her mother did that, her mother's mother probably did that, too. I thought giving up everything would make me a better mother, but truthfully it made me worse. I was miserable living my life only for my children. This is, again, the part where it's important to stress that I love my children to death; it's the crippling pressures of being the perfect parent I did not love that left me miserable.

MOMS COME FIRST.

My mother raised two little girls on her own, working two jobs, and she made it look effortless. She wasn't hiding her struggles to be the perfect mom, she was just doing what she had to do to get by, to survive, to keep us safe and happy. She didn't fall victim to the perfection expectations, because she was alone most of the time and had no killjoy social media comparisons. It was my mom who gave me the support to be a just-average mom.

My grandma was the opposite; she led me to believe my children would "complete me." That I had to give up all the things to put my children first.

But moms come first.

This is breaking intergenerational cycles at its finest.

My toddler went through a rough period when he was waking up every night and it would take us all hours of crying to get back to sleep. That's when I introduced the floor bed.

A great friend of mine who is a sleep consultant told me sometimes you have to get creative when it comes to sleep and toddlers. She mentioned something about letting them sleep on the floor next to me, which meant I would still get sleep and so would they. Win-win. I never would have thought I'd be that mom. But we are all sleeping and with minimal disturbances. Now I know it's a phase, and we will get him back to sleeping in his bed when it's time, and we will all know when it's time. You just have to trust your gut, not your head.

So fuck it, break the rules from time to time.

The truth is, there isn't an area of motherhood that is not hard at one point or another. If you let your kids sleep in your room to avoid fighting now, that just means you'll be dealing with a transition later, and that's okay. The point is, you get to pick your hard.

It's your choice what rules you break and bend. If you don't know how to tell if you're doing the right thing or not, just ask yourself:
1. Is this hurting anyone?
2. Am I good with this? Meaning, can I live with this for a little while?
3. Is it sustainable?

Another pre-parenthood rule of mine was the screen time and iPad dilemma. I never actually bought an iPad for my toddler, he just claimed mine for his own. We are so quick to judge moms who use screens to get through dinner at a restaurant, but those moms are just doing what they can to get through a meal without a total meltdown. Now that I've been there and done that, I almost respect those moms even more for knowing what they needed to do. It's just a meal! They're not making their children eat crumbs off the floor. Honestly, if no

iPad means the children are going to be screaming instead, I'm doubly thankful.

We are all trying to survive each day. The rules we break and bend are just so we can make it till bedtime without losing our cool. We break the rules because we need a break, too. TV time can be a great moment to collect yourself and regroup till bedtime.

We think we can do it better than everyone else before we have kids, and then quickly realize that it's not a competition. We end up on the struggle bus like every other mom.

Take the kids to the drive-through, if it means you don't stress about dinner and cleanup tonight. Let them play on the screens, if it means you get some much-needed quiet time to recharge and rally for the bedtime routine. Let them wear the ridiculous Paw Patrol shoes, because they are the kids. Let them sleep in your room, if it's what you want to do, and it means you'll get a little extra sleep at night.

They truly are only this little for such a small amount of time. You are their safe place, that's why they come to you.

Get rid of the rules you made for yourself that no longer serve you.

They are your rules, Mama. You are allowed to break them.

IF YOU HAVE A BABY, YOU ARE A MAMA

There is no right way or wrong way to have a baby. Whether that is by C-section, via adoption, vaginally, in a bathtub, or on a bus. The way a baby is brought into the world is not something that we should carry with shame. We all know that's only the beginning of the real shitshow anyways. The fact that they made it here truly is the treasure, not the boat on which the baby came into our lives.

We talk about our birth stories because it's fun to relive these

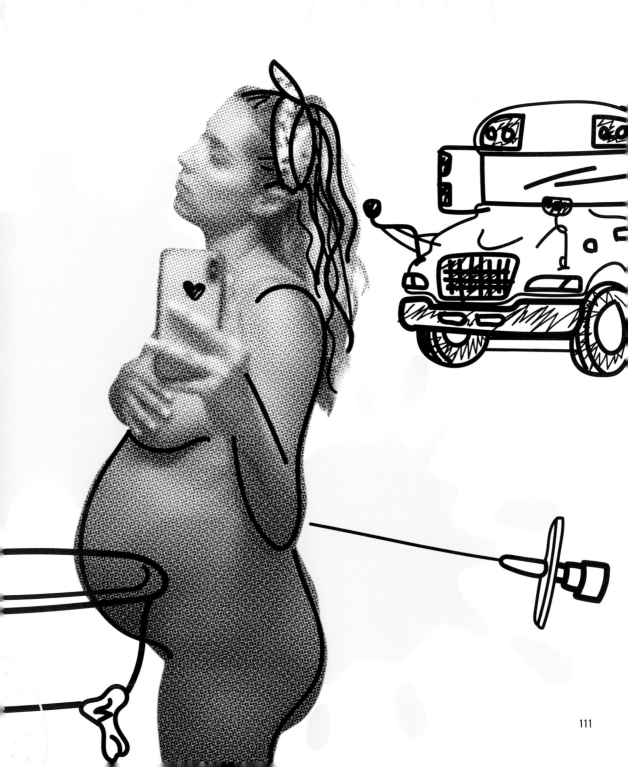

THERE IS NO RIGHT WAY OR WRONG WAY TO HAVE A BABY. WHETHER THAT IS BY C-SECTION, VIA ADOPTION, VAGINALLY, IN A BATHTUB, OR ON A BUS.

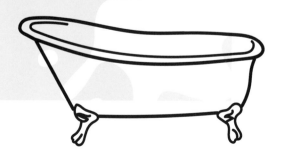

moments; and it's really easy to get caught up in comparison, in how you wished it had gone versus what happened. But nonetheless, you are a mom. You won't always be talking about your vagina with strangers. (Well, maybe. It's just more common when the babies are little and can't get too embarrassed yet.)

With my first child, I had so many visitors, and I was so tired by the time the baby would take a nap—and I desperately needed one, too—but then someone else would show up. The second time, I said hell no. I wanted to be alone, to recover and rest. I knew that once I got home I had two children to take care of. Also, lying in a bed all day is a dream vacation for most moms.

The funny part about bringing a child into your life, whether vaginally, by C-section, or through adoption, is it may be the first and last time we realize we have (little to) no control over the hardest things in life. And no control is what we need to learn to live with to get through the mom life.

BEING A MOTHER IS A CHOICE (ALLEGEDLY) WE MAKE EVERY SINGLE DAY. YOU ARE A MOTHER BECAUSE YOU WANT TO BE ONE.

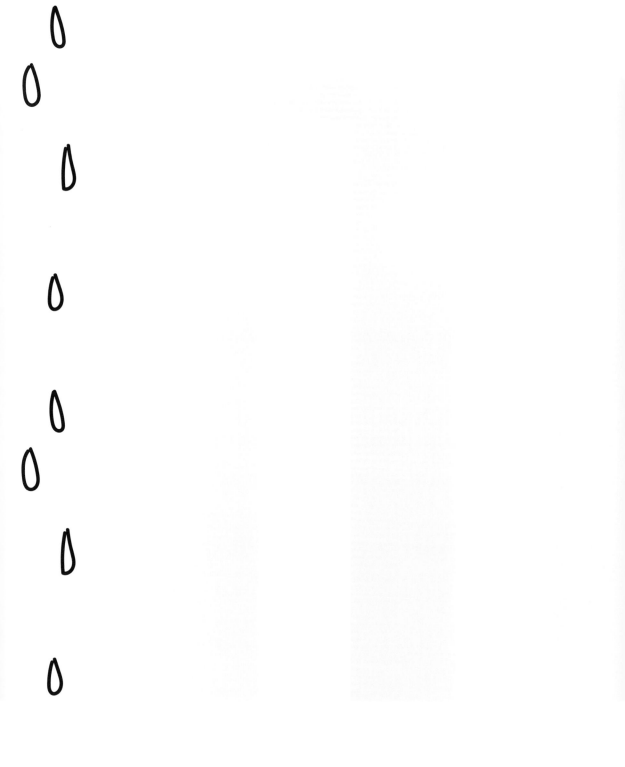

THERE WILL BE CRYING...

TEARS

When I first became a mother, I would measure how great my days were based on how much crying there was. Looking back, it seems silly. Yet parenting is just too easy to take personally, right? Our babies do not actually hate us; teens maybe, but babies? No way.

They are crying because they want us closer. They feel safe in our arms. Yes, we have to put the baby down to take a shower and cook dinner from time to time, so they are probably a little pissed about that. But they don't hate you. They love you. They will always love you.

The crying doesn't mean you are a bad mom. It's the only way they know how to communicate. Unfortunately for us, we don't speak crying baby, so sometimes we misunderstand their needs. Babies will cry because they are hungry, uncomfortable, or just need extra cuddles. Or sometimes it'll feel like for no reason at all.

IS IT STILL UNSETTLING? I'VE NEVER BEEN MORE UNSETTLED IN MY LIFE THAN WHEN MY CHILD IS CRYING.

Does it also make me want to cry? Sometimes! I feel so triggered when my kids cry. It's hard not to get emotional myself; it's normal to feel this way. As mothers, we are meant to react to our children's cries. Biology, baby.

Trust your motherly instincts, and if you think you need to take the baby to the doctor, do it. It's far better for them to send you home after telling you there's nothing wrong than to wait and kill yourself with worry. Trust me, I've been there more times than I'd like to admit, but I

always felt better on the car ride home knowing I did my best.

I wish someone had told me that it's okay to put them down and give yourself a minute to collect yourself before you get back to the soothing. We can try our best, but sometimes we can't fix all the problems, all the time. There will be crying and we just have to do our best to get through it.

With my second, I would place him in his swing and just hold my hand on him until he calmed down. By contrast, when my first would cry, I would put him in his baby carrier and dance around the living room for fifteen minutes to get him to either fall asleep or just calm down, but I couldn't keep it up. **My neck, my back, my feet couldn't take it anymore. The bigger the baby, the bigger the back pain.**

Thankfully, time flies when you are taking care of very demanding little humans, and the more they can speak, the more they can tell you what they are upset about. Which can sometimes be really annoying.

What happens when the kids are a little older and the crying newborn turns into a crying toddler? I've had multiple conversations with therapists and child-rearing experts, and they all say the same thing: validation of your children's emotions comes first.

We wouldn't want to stop our children laughing, so the goal is to understand why they are crying and help them through their big emotions. We don't want to tell them, "Don't cry," because we all cry from time to time; it's a release, it's okay to cry.

Emotions come and go; suppressing them in our children (and ourselves) is not a healthy coping mechanism. Emotions just *are*. We are happy, we are sad. The good news is that feelings are temporary, happy or sad. Being present with our children during big emotions and validating their feelings is the best way to help them feel seen and heard. What this does is help them process and move on, just like it does for us.

A good friend once told me, in regard to kids and feelings, "What goes up must come down." When you have a big, exciting day, you eventually fall flat on your face, because excitement is exhausting. The same holds true for kids. So when you have that big Disney trip planned, what goes up will always come down. It's part of the rollercoaster of motherhood.

Friendly Reminder, Mama: Try your best not to beat yourself up about having a meltdown; the same holds true for your children. We are only human, and big emotions will never actually leave us, and that's 100,000 percent okay. Moms are like pressure cookers: you gotta let a little steam out so the lid doesn't pop off.

We bear the weight of the world on our shoulders; no wonder we melt from time to time. We are allowed to feel, express, release, and if we hurt anyone in the process, apologize. When I say hurt, I don't mean physical harm.

The truth is, we all will lose our cool. The difference is how we handle it afterward. It takes a self-aware mama to admit when she was wrong and validate the feelings of her children. We can promise to try better next time—if we mean it—or just acknowledge that Mommy was having a hard time, like we all do, and she's sorry for yelling.

Modeling the behavior we want to see in our children is key. They learn less by what we say and more from what we do, especially when no one is looking.

MOTHERHOOD IS DRAINING ON THE BEST OF DAYS, AND IT SURE AS SHIT IS DRAINING ON THE WORST OF DAYS.

ALL THE FEELS

Motherhood makes you feel everything and anything all at once. You feel happy when your kids are awake, but sad because you wanted some more alone time. Happy to get away to go to the store, but worried about them the whole time you're there.

As moms, we now feel the emotions of our children, partners, and anyone else close by. We somehow wear the emotions of everyone we know and love. Exhausting, right?

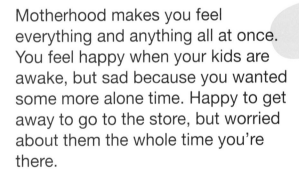

As a new mom, I felt drained from feeling all the things, all the time. What helped me the most was first identifying what I was feeling. Was I feeling anxious? Was I feeling sad? Was I feeling jealous that my partner went to work and didn't have to change 1,000 diapers a day?

Once you identify the feeling, then you can take action to help process it. Ask yourself, *How can I feel less anxious? What can I do to bring myself a little joy?*

When I feel anxious, I listen to a mindfulness meditation, practice breathing techniques, and take a nice, long, hot bath. If I'm feeling down, I try listening to my favorite songs for a quick pick-me-up. If I'm jealous that my partner went to work and doesn't have to change shit diapers today, I try planning a date for myself and friends.

LISTEN TO YOURSELF AND DO WHAT YOU NEED TO DO. NO ONE IS GOING TO FIGURE THIS STUFF OUT FOR YOU, UNFORTUNATELY.

The only way to truly replenish yourself is to figure out what fills your cup. Figure out what works for you—reading a book, working out, anything that gives your mind a minute to forget about the grocery shopping and the monthly to-do lists.

It's truly important for you to figure out what fills you up so you can turn to these things when you feel empty. Sometimes cleaning with loud music does this for me, but this doesn't work every day. Sometimes I'll need more of a break, like getting my nails done, or that nice hot bath.

If you still don't know what works for you, try a whole bunch of new things and see which energized you and which depleted you. Different things work for different people. You owe it to yourself to figure out what works for you.

YOU CAN'T AND SHOULDN'T DO IT ALL

Hear me out. Maybe you *can* do everything, but that doesn't mean you should. There will be days when the laundry piles up, but the kids have an engaged and fun mom; then there will be days you do the laundry and feel more like a zombie. We think we must do it all at once, and then blame ourselves when we can't.

"Doing it all" doesn't come with a trophy, a large lump sum of money, or extra paid vacation days. Although for some reason, I still felt I needed to do it all—to prove what? To whom?

As a new mom, I thought doing it all made me a good mom and wife. Cook dinner, clean the kitchen, get the kids ready for bed, each and every single step in the process. I thought that if I could act the way I saw the moms in commercials act, I'd experience the satisfaction they all seemed to feel as well. Maybe I thought it meant my kids would love me more, my family would be proud of me, but I was the one suffering.

It took me almost a year to even feel comfortable asking Grandma to watch the kids so I could take care of X, Y, or Z.

We are not meant to do it all every day. Some moms are lucky enough to have someone help with cleaning or watching the kids so they can shower. But not all. For those moms flying solo-ish, which is so many of us, we must pace ourselves. Parenting isn't done in a day. It's a process of days, weeks, months, and years. It's a 100K, not a marathon. Pace yourself.

Have you ever heard of the glass and plastic ball analogy? To sum it up, moms are constantly juggling glass and plastic balls, and it's up to you to figure out which balls are made of glass and which are made of plastic. When you drop a plastic ball, sure, you "dropped the ball," but it's plastic, so it'll bounce back and won't break. The glass ones will break and will not be replaceable. So is your glass ball cooking a three-course meal tonight? Probably not.

The kids will be just fine if you order pizza. A glass ball is remembering to pick up your kids from school on time. Prioritize what's important for the day and acknowledge which balls can be dropped without shattering.

As parents, our plates are always full (and most likely cold). Figuring out what you can delegate is key to survival, and getting your partner on board is crucial. Splitting up chores in the house, hiring help in the areas you are able, all help you to help yourself.

Some days I prioritize myself, take a shower, blow-dry my hair, and fill my cup. Other days, I take the kids to the zoo in 100-degree weather and hate life. It's all about balance. Some days I scream at my partner, some days at my kids. See? Balance.

It's important for your kids to see you doing things you love. That they see you enjoy life and understand that they are not the center of the universe. (Although they are the center of yours.) That way, when they go out into the real world someday, they won't have to spend a lot of time adjusting their expectations...or in therapy.

TIME FOR A CHANGE.

We do not live in a generation where our "village" comes and helps clean and cook when a new child arrives; so how do we create a village experience? We identify and delegate.

Just because you were born with a uterus (or if you are the default parent) this does not mean you love cooking, cleaning, and caring for the kids 24/7, with no support. Of course, some of us love parts of the madness, but I'm here to tell you that if you don't fit into the traditional mold of what it means to be a woman, you're not alone, and for good reason.

Why is it that (some) men think they are too good for housework? **Sorry, honey, it's time for you to get your ass up.**

Only we can demand change under our roof, so whatever is not working for you, make him do it. We were not born to be the housekeepers of our family. Just because he was born with a penis doesn't mean he can't do the dishes.

I personally can't for the life of me stay on top of laundry. I know it's rather cliché and a topic for most mom jokes, but it truly brings me anxiety, and I'll spend half a day putting clothes away that I want to set on fire. I decided for my own mental health and for the sake of my family that I would pay someone to help me clean our clothes. Can we really afford it? It's cutting it close, but that gives me more time to work and more time to spend with the kids. I will gladly pay someone so I don't have to touch the Mt. Everest of dread.

And finally, day care. Oh, my love for day care. When I first pushed out my crotch goblin, I vowed to be a stay-at-home mom forever. Eventually I figured out that I needed more help than the couple hours a week my family would come over. Putting my children in day care was a choice I made for myself, but it has benefited my kids more than I could have ever dreamed. This is the help I wish for every mom who can afford it. Also, we put this on a credit card because living with a burnt-out mom is not a price my kids should have to pay.

It's so easy to get caught up in what we "should" be doing rather than what's really important. Our children will not care about the cleanliness of the house or what you cooked for dinner. What they do care about is your presence, how you make them feel.

IF WE DON'T LABEL MEN LAZY FOR NOT CLEANING, COOKING, OR CARING FOR CHILDREN, THEN WE DO NOT NEED TO ASSIGN THOSE LABELS TO OURSELVES.

YOU ARE HEREBY FOUND NOT GUILTY

I came up with a great way to treat mom guilt. Now, this isn't going to be a one-and-done type of cure. It will take practice and constant exercising to help build your mom-guilt-free muscles. This is just a mental workout, because screw actual working out, who has energy for that shit?

I've named it the "replacement method." It has worked wonders for me, and I hope some version of it can work for you. It goes like this: when intrusive thoughts of mom guilt bubble up, you must first take a deep breath and then consciously stop the thought and replace it with a sentence like "I'm doing the best I can."

Kiss guilt

mom
goodbye

When you feel uneasy, question yourself: *Why?* Most of the time, it's because of some narrative we are telling ourselves about the past or future that we cannot control.

We are going to make mistakes; we are going to feel inadequate from time to time. How we speak to ourselves is the only difference between mom guilt and forgiveness.

When you need a reminder or your thoughts and insecurities are spiraling, remember to repeat after me:

I will not feel guilty for things I can't control.
I will not feel guilty because I don't mom the way other moms do.
I will not feel guilty for taking time for myself; I fucking deserve it.
I will not feel guilty for doing something that makes me happy.
I will not feel guilty for asking for what I need.
I will not feel guilty for prioritizing my needs.
I am doing the best I can.
I am doing what works best for me.
I am a great mom.
I am a great woman.
It's okay to have bad days. It doesn't make me a bad mom.

This is your life, this is your time to enjoy what you can, while you can.

So go get your hair done, go out to dinner with friends; it's still your life, too. Do the things that make you happy. Just make sure your kids are in the safest environment possible. We cannot control all outcomes, no matter how much we try.

You do not need to feel guilty because other moms do things differently than you. **Your worth is not determined by how other moms mother their children.**

EVERYONE ON SOCIAL MEDIA IS SHOWING THEIR HIGHLIGHT REEL ANYWAYS, IT'S NOT REAL LIFE.

losing yourself

Don't worry if you've lost yourself, because moms are the best at finding things. I think we are meant to lose ourselves in motherhood. It's the rebirth of you as a human. You must unlearn everything you've ever known, and get reacquainted with the world through the eyes of someone new. By no means is this easy. When you go from 0 to 1,000 mph in a matter of 24 hours, it's heavy, it's debilitating, and it's soul crushing.

This is to say that even if you're feeling lost, you are where you're supposed to be, for now. Don't worry, it's only temporary.

Then

Now

A new chapter of your life is beginning, and you can't take all your old habits and beliefs into it. Otherwise, there will be no room for growth.

You get to decide where you want to go from here. Moms don't have a lot of spare time, so this is when you decide how to use it wisely. Do you really want to go to dinner with that acquaintance and miss out on sleep? Do you want to go get a massage or get your hair done? You're forced to choose between options constantly, and it's through making these choices that you will find the new you.

Motherhood is one of the most life-changing conditions that you can willingly* sign up for.

*I say that with an asterisk because we often really don't know what we are getting ourselves into until it's too late, and unfortunately there's no undo button. (Kidding—sort of.)

Sometimes we reconnect with parts of ourselves that existed pre-children on an even deeper level. For example, I knew I was social, but I didn't realize how much I need some adult social contact until it was completely missing from my life. I also **love** dancing—as in, I can get *less* sleep because I went out dancing, and still feel *more* energized the next day because I did something for myself. I didn't realize this until after kids; it was so easy to do these things before, I took them for granted. Now, I have to plan for them, but it's worth it.

There will be a lot of things that no longer serve the new you because you've changed. Your brain has changed, your family has changed, and your friends have changed. You are seeing life through a whole new perspective, and that's normal. It's scary at first because you're not sure what to do with yourself: how to think, or how to feel about it. There is no rush. You have the rest of your life to figure yourself out, again. Little by little, day by day, and it will still change over time. Give yourself permission to change. We are supposed to.

Losing myself was the best thing that happened to me. Giving birth to my kids led me to the rebirth of myself—I actually have a snake tattoo that signifies this. When you live a life of people pleasing, it's easy to be unsure of what you want, because other people's opinions matter more to you than your own. For example, I wanted to please my husband, but I eventually realized that was not the same as pleasing myself. I wanted my family to be proud of me, but sometimes the things I did to achieve that only took me further away from my true self.

As women, we are often taught that putting ourselves last is selfless and part of what it means to be a good mom. And this is how it starts; by subjugating

ourselves, we teach our children to seek external approval rather than their own. This can mean different things for different people—I know for me, this meant losing whole swaths of my identity. When I came out, I was finally choosing to stand with myself above anyone else. And just as important, I was showing my children that it's never too late to find yourself. I wanted to be an example of how, if we choose to live our lives authentically, the rest will fall into place. In leading by example, I have taught my children to be accepting of others, not just about sexual identity, but also about what a family can look like. I wanted my kids to know firsthand that they already have my acceptance and to give them the opportunity to ask themselves the same questions, with my loving support.

If we try too hard to hang on to who we were before we became parents, we might miss out on our own growth. This doesn't mean we're not allowed to miss parts of our old lives. I miss the freedom, the ability to just pick up and go wherever I wanted, whenever I wanted. I miss sitting. I miss being in control of only me. I miss being able to stay out late, and then stay in bed the next day. It's okay to miss the old you. We all feel it from time to time. It doesn't mean you don't love your children, or that you are a bad mom, I promise.

Ironically, these days when I'm presented with some freedom, I often don't even know what to do with myself. I don't really want to stay out all hours of the night. If I had to pick sleep or dancing, nine times out of ten I'm going to pick sleep. Motherhood breaks you down to a shell of a human and then slowly builds you back up into a fuller, more robust version of you. We don't have time to fuck around, our time is precious. Maybe the lack of sleep helps us set boundaries we never knew we needed. Moms simply don't have the time to waste on bullshit.

Be kind with yourself, be open with your mind, and be generous with your grace, because you deserve that. You deserve the evolution and silver linings that come with motherhood.

You'll question yourself. Which is okay in moderation.

You'll question society. Which is a great gift to teach your children.

You'll question your marriage. Which will help you two either grow closer or further apart.

You'll question everything and that's okay.

Do I really want to go to a restaurant with a bunch of friends and fight my child the whole time and leave flustered without having had a single bite to eat? Nah. Do I want to take them to an indoor playground where I can happily sit on my phone and drink coffee while they play independently in a safe area? Yes. Maybe it's the opposite feeling for you, and that's fine, too.

These moments of self-reflection and assessment will tell you what pleases you and how to find yourself again.

Losing yourself allows you to figure out what truly makes you happy. Because when a child is born, so is a mother.

LOSING YOURSELF ALLOWS YOU TO FIGURE OUT WHAT TRULY MAKES YOU HAPPY. BECAUSE WHEN A CHILD IS BORN, SO IS A MOTHER.

FEELING THE BURNOUT?

What does mom burnout feel like? You've got a short fuse, you're exhausted, and you feel empty inside. You've lost interest in things that used to interest you, food can taste bland, and life feels dull. You hate everyone and everything.

Your signs may be different from mine, but when I start dreading picking up my kids from school, I know I need a break.

Mom life can feel overwhelming or near impossible at times. Some of us don't have family to lean on, or the finances for outside help. And how do we find a babysitter we trust? It feels like hurdle after hurdle.

INSTEAD OF MISSING OUT ON THE THINGS I LOVE, I DECIDED TO DO THEM, TIRED.

Let's say you're lucky enough to find the sitter and the money to go have an adult playdate; now you must plan and prepare everything before you leave. Let's not forget the anxiety and worry about leaving our children. The guilt can boil over so quickly, and we feel like we are being selfish for wanting anything for ourselves.

I'm here to promise and remind you, we are better mothers after a break. Getting away, even for dinner with friends, can be enough to fill that cup. It's not like you're leaving your kids forever; it's a weekend, an evening, an hour. They will be all right.

When you're already tired, sometimes making "fun" plans sounds like just one more exhausting thing to do. Yes, you'll be tired, but do the damn thing anyways. When you start laughing and having a good time, your body will get a natural boost that's better than any $7 cup of coffee. It took me a long time to realize that I was going to be tired no matter what. Instead of missing out on the things I love, I decided to do them, tired.

I can probably count on one hand how many times I went out to dinner with friends after our first kid. It took me four years to have my first kid-free weekend away. You may be thinking: why the hell did it take me that long? With my first child, we were exclusively breastfeeding, so I had to always be nearby. Plus, with the crippling postpartum anxiety, I just couldn't bring myself to let go. Leaving your kids for the first time, you feel like you might actually die.

Well, at least, I did. My second child came around, and then the whole world closed because of the pandemic; I was too terrified to leave my house.

A few months into lockdown, I booked a weekend away with my two best friends; it was helpful to have something to look forward to, something to think about and plan that had nothing to do with motherhood. It was a nice break for my mind leading up to the trip, and then the day before, I broke. I snapped. The pressure of making sure everything was perfect before I left and the anxiety of leaving my kids got to me. I just had to keep reminding myself that they would be fine, and that I needed this.

THE TIME AWAY FROM YOUR KIDS IS MINIMAL COMPARED TO THE TIME YOU SPEND WITH THEM FEELING BURNT OUT.

You know what happened when I got home from my first weekend trip? The kids didn't even act like I had left. I had been overly obsessing, thinking, worrying, that they would think I was gone for good. I was so excited to pick up my younger son from his nap after I came home, and he literally acted like I had never even left.

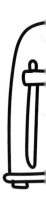

Moral of the story is that we love our children, and we never want to do anything that will make them feel like we love them any less. I'm here to tell you that a short trip away is not going to make them feel abandoned. The fact that you worry about leaving them proves how much you love them, and they feel that. Trust me.

And for those who weren't worried and were already taking time away? There's nothing wrong with you, either.

Let's say that going away is just out of the question; how do we replenish ourselves with our children around? For starters, we have to identify what fills us up. When I need a break from routine but I can't run away, we do ice cream for dinner. It won't kill them, I promise.

The looks on their faces, the excitement, the break from the mundane, from the fights over dinner, it's a break we take together. For a brief moment, we are all happy, and that in itself is replenishing.

The first step to fixing anything is figuring out that there's something that needs fixing.

You've got this, Mama.

YOU DON'T NEED A BREAKDOWN *breakdown* TO DESERVE A BREAK

For so many generations, women were encouraged to swallow their feelings and hide their struggles. Breaking generational cycles is hard, even harder if we don't notice we're caught in one.

When we complain about motherhood to our mothers, some might say, "It's just the way it is." Maybe even "You signed up for this." They say it without realizing they're just repeating the feedback they received as new moms. When they were in your position, no one was talking about self-care or normalizing that moms need breaks, too. That we can want and need more outside of motherhood.

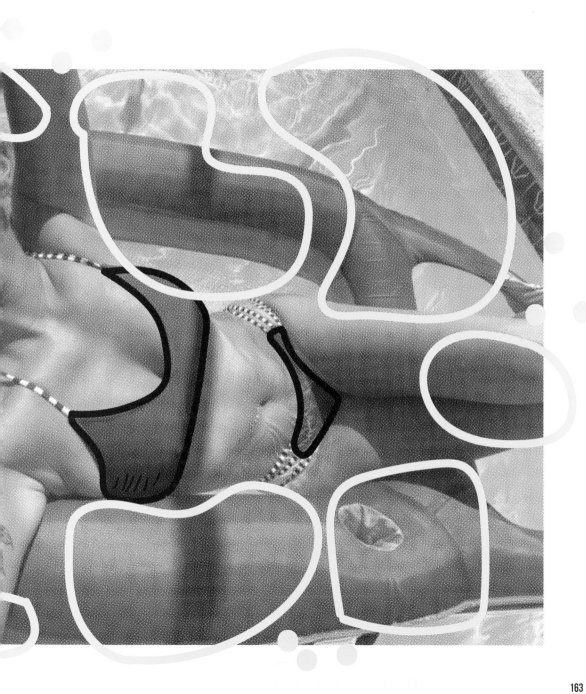

We no longer have to hide our pain; we can seek help. We don't have to suffer.

The pain we feel inside our hearts and minds is a call that needs to be answered. We don't have to suppress it anymore. Our emotions and feelings are not a weakness, but a strength. We are not emotional, we are feeling emotions.

If you need a break, take it.
You'll be a better mom for it.

If you need meds, take them.
You'll be a better mom for it.

If you need therapy, do it.
You'll be a better mom for it.

If you need help getting your baby to sleep, do it.
You'll be a better mom for it.

If you need to cry, do it.
You'll be a better mom for it.

Times have changed, and sometimes, the advice needs to, too. You don't have to suffer through this chapter of life because your parents and grandparents did. We have more resources today than they did back then, so let's use them. Being a fulfilled mom will always make us a better mom.

YOU DON'T NEED TO LOOK LIKE A MOM

There's no such thing as looking like a mom; there are two billion moms on this planet and that number grows by the second. Which means there are two billion ways to look like a mom.

I wanted to dress the part. I've always loved dressing up. I wore the pretty button-down blouses, the long blonde hair; I took out my nose ring and stopped daydreaming of my next tattoo, because I thought that's what I had to do.

Maybe I thought dressing "like a mom" would make me feel like a better mom or even feel more mom-ish, because clearly, I was struggling, like most of us do. I was really

169

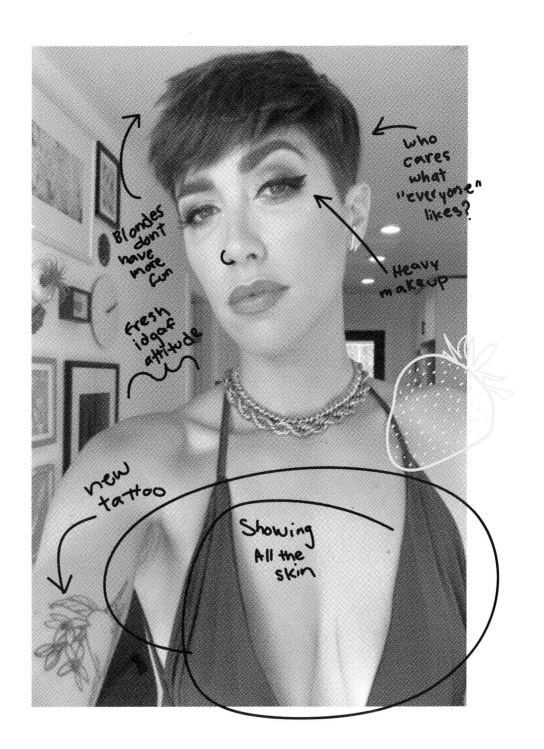

looking for acceptance from myself. Eventually I realized I was just trying to fit into a mold that wasn't made for me. The need to be my own creative self never went away, so I ended up repiercing my nose, cutting off all my hair, and getting more tattoos, because life is too short not to be yourself. If you can't be yourself, who can you be?

Back to mom: you're the same person you were before you had kids, now you just have kids. So, dress the way you want, dye your hair, pierce your nose, get the tattoos. No one is stopping you.

What's beautiful is that this proves to our children that they too can be who they want. They can live authentically, and they don't have to conform.

There's not much happiness that can come from trying to live our lives to impress anyone but ourselves.

YAY, POTTY TRAINING! SAID NO MOM EVER

Here's the thing that all the books, professionals, and bloggers try to tell you: GO BIG OR GO HOME with potty training. Like the three-day potty-training method, which means everything in your house will be covered in piss, oh how delightful.

Now, this approach certainly works, but you don't have to go balls to the wall (no pun intended) to get your child potty trained. You can work on this a couple hours a day, as you see fit. No potty-training police will come after you, I promise. Does this slow down the process a little? Sure. But it also lessens the stress and anxiety of potty training.

YOU JUST HAVE TO DO IT WHEN YOU ARE READY. IT'S GOING TO BE MESSY, NO MATTER WHAT.

As if we aren't busy and stressed enough already. Just add a pissing and shitting naked child running around the house to spice things up.

I potty trained my son around two while I was stuck at home feeling very pregnant with my second baby. We did the three days of being naked so he could start to realize what that urge to go looks and feels like, but after that, we practiced when I had time and the mental capacity to handle it.

Like *all* things in motherhood, it's never one size fits all. You'll know what's working and what's not after a couple days.

The other thing I tell all my friends with kids is that *you* have to be ready to potty train. Don't feel pressured by some internet search on "when should my kid be potty trained?" Sure, the child needs to be "ready," too. I tried potty training too early, because we were going on a cruise and the rule was no swim diapers in the pools, but neither of us was ready.

They do potty train kids sooner in other countries, but depending on your level of support, work schedule, or mental load…sooner may not work for you. You just have to do it when you are ready. It's going to be messy, no matter what.

NAP

LIFE

nap life

If you count down the minutes till naptime or bedtime, you're not alone. I have this love-hate relationship with naps. I love when they are sleeping, but hate the mental prep work to get there; and just when you think you've got it all figured out, their sleep schedule changes.

I remember thinking that after I sleep trained at four months, I was "finished." *cries in sleep deprivation*

My biggest takeaway from *somewhat* surviving child sleep habits is that

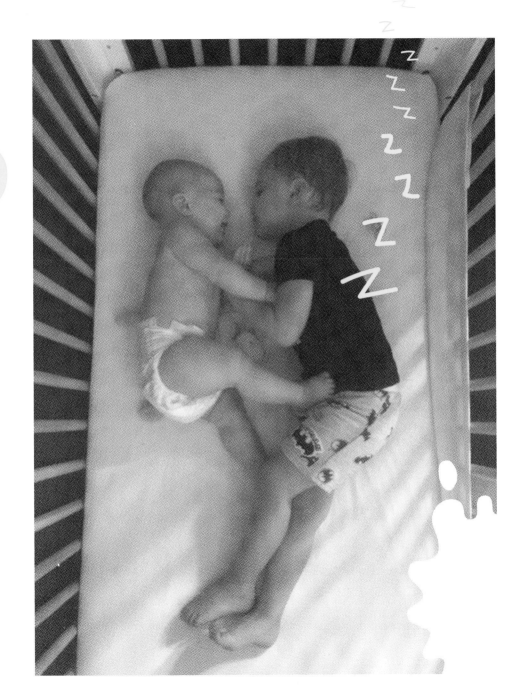

you have to be flexible, and that there are recommended wake windows for every age group; but also, take that with a grain of salt, because our kids love breaking and bending and challenging any and all rules.

So what do you do during naps or bedtime?

Do you clean? Catch up on Netflix? Scroll through social media? Stare at the wall and question what the fuck have you done with your life? No matter what you decide to do, you'll wish you were doing the other. That's the motherhood paradox for you.

I always try to do something I "couldn't" do while the kids are awake, like **sitting.** Gosh, I never realized how much I love sitting until my kids literally wouldn't let me sit down.

The real never-ending story is our to-do list; but resting ourselves should be on there, too. Resting is productive. Doing nothing is also productive. We need these little moments to recharge. Some days you'll feel like tackling the 2.5 million loads of laundry (allegedly), and some days you'll need to sit on the couch and be a vegetable. Both are productive.

Do you ever take a moment to chill out on the couch but are still going over the list of things you "should" be doing in your head, and then wonder why you don't feel rested? You need to give yourself full permission to relax, physically and mentally.

Or just take a nap yourself, drool and all.

Motherhood is like a high-intensity sport; treat it as one.

REST AND RECOVER.

nap so hard

SUPPORT IS NOT JUST FOR BRAS

BEING SUPPORTIVE IS NOT LIMITED TO ONLY SUPPORTING THE OTHER MOMS WHO DO THINGS THE SAME AS YOU.

Please read that again.

There's a whole new wave of online confrontation, something our parents' generation never had to deal with. We need to come to a better understanding of what it means to be a supportive fellow mama. Motherhood is a sisterhood, and we can't fuck this shit up with hate.

Fighting about who parents better is just a waste of time when you realize we are all doing the best we can. That doing "our best" will look different for different moms.

Maybe she (and I mean me) goes to the drive-through, because she doesn't have the energy to cook a dinner none of her children will eat. Now, unless you plan on coming over, cooking, *and* cleaning up the mess, you can keep your opinions to yourself. Your opinion is just that: an opinion.

We could help each other more and fight less. We could openly communicate more and stop calling each other names. We could support each other more and hate less. We won't be able to understand every mother's choices, because we are not every mother. We can have similar stories and upbringings, but we can still choose different ways to parent our children. We are different.

How boring would it be if we all did things the same exact way, right?

We will learn from each other more if we can just give each other a little bit more grace, and a lot less hate and judgment.

This is not a game show where the best mom wins 28 million dollars and a new dishwasher. It's not a competition. I know this sounds cliché, but why else would we be tearing each other down? To be at the top? To win? To be the best? What prize do we come away with, Top Mom? FFS.

Moms judge each other for how we choose to get our babies to sleep, what they eat, if they go to day care, or if they stay home. You get the point. We are all just trying to survive. Who made you or me the judge of anyone else's hard road through this mom life?

The next time you take umbrage with someone doing things differently than you, ask yourself why it bothers you.

Is it because you fought so hard to limit screen time that when someone else lets their kids watch it freely, it upsets you? Maybe that mom is fighting hard for her mental health, and realized that a little screen time was better than being a distant, burnt-out mom.

Your worth is not defined by how other women mother their children.

Maybe your kid stays over at someone else's house, and they have different rules. So be it. We can't control everything. Our kid will survive a night with cereal for dinner and too much TV. We all did.

We are allowed to do things differently and still be supportive of each other.

WHEN YOU KNOW, YOU KNOW

For many reasons, this is a taboo subject: You're not supposed to ask another woman if she's going to have more kids. So who can we ask about how to know when we are done having them?

Me. You can ask me.

When my second child came into the picture, I enjoyed it so much more than the first round. Not because he was a better baby, but because I was a more experienced and relaxed mama. I no longer had postpartum

anxiety. I almost didn't want it to end—I would cry at the thought that he was my last baby. Possibly the hormones are to blame. I quit breastfeeding when I wanted to, I felt more comfortable about naps and letting others hold him (which I know sounds weird but if you have any PPA/PPD, you know). It just felt the way I thought motherhood was supposed to feel. So that made me question if I was truly done having kids. How would I know?

I knew I wanted a second child when my first was just over a year old. I would see a baby and it would literally bring me to tears. I would see a pregnant woman and feel jealousy in my soul because I wanted to be pregnant, too. The pull was there, and it was the only thing I could think about—damn hormones. I was waiting for that same feeling to come after my second before I made any big decisions.

The year mark passed us right by, and when a friend of mine told me she was expecting, I was happy for her, but I knew (for the first time) I didn't want that for myself. The idea of starting over made me anxious. I really felt like I was finally finding my individuality. The freedom I have now, emotionally and mentally, was something I was not ready to sacrifice. I didn't want to give up sleeping, have gestational diabetes, or breastfeed again. I truthfully didn't want any part of doing it once more.

This doesn't mean I don't still love babies. I think when you love babies, you'll always love babies. If you had a decent experience with those beginning years, you'll maybe get teary when a baby makes eye contact or smiles at you. That may not mean you *need* another baby. (And you can always borrow one if that urge is strong.)

My answer didn't come to me overnight either, it took weeks of thinking about it. So if you are unsure, give yourself some time to figure it out.

VENTING ISN'T JUST FOR AIR CONDITIONERS (OR, YOU'RE ALLOWED TO COMPLAIN)

Fruits of Motherhood
@fruitsofruits

Sorry I didn't text you back, I
probably opened the text message
and in that exact moment my child
tried to jump off the back of the
couch onto the dining room table
and then probably started
demanding snacks.

Fruits of Motherhood
@fruitsofruits

Motherhood is waking up feeling like
you were hit by a truck and going to
sleep feeling like you were hit by 2.
Repeat.

I had a family member say to me, *Why do you complain about your kids all the time on the internet?* Me? Complaining? I reread all my posts with that in mind and still couldn't see what she was talking about. Then it hit me; I wasn't complaining, I was being honest. She came from a generation where swallowing your hardships and smiling through them without saying a peep was the norm, the expectation. Women were not allowed to say anything negative about motherhood, let alone on a public platform for everyone to see—including our children someday. *GASP!*

Fruits of Motherhood
@lindafruits

Cheers to never needing an alarm
clock ever again after having
children. If they don't wake me up,
the stress of them not waking me up
does.

 **Fruits of Motherhood**
@lindafruits

Being a mom is understanding that
things in your house just take turns
being clean. The kitchen, the
children, the dining room table or
your hair. Can't have it all.

 **Fruits of Motherhood**
@lindafruits

Motherhood feels overstimulating
and under-stimulating. Like you
never have enough energy but also
can never seem to relax. It's
simultaneously feeling like you've
given your all and yet it feels like you
could have done more. Just know at
the end of the day mama, you are
enough.

I've never loved a single
human so much in my
entire life and I've also
never been so excited for
7:30pm in my entire life.

@fruitsofmotherhood

 Fruits of Motherhood
@lindafruits

I didn't realize how much I loved
sitting and doing nothing until I had
kids and they wouldn't let me sit and
do nothing.

 Fruits of Motherhood
@lindafruits

Motherhood is fun because you try
to just survive the day and then
once they go to sleep you question
yourself why you didn't do more.

DON'T ASK MOMS WHAT
WE LIKE TO DO FOR FUN
BECAUSE I'M GOING TO SAY
SOMETHING LIKE SITTING
ON THE COUCH STARING AT
THE WALL AND I DON'T
WANT TO MAKE IT WEIRD.

@FRUITSOFMOTHERHOOD

 Fruits of Motherhood
@lindafruits

Welcome to motherhood.
You sleep like shit.
Feel like shit.
Tired of everybody's shit.
But you love those little shits.

The previous generations sugarcoated motherhood so heavily that by the time we got through the layers of frosting, we felt lost, betrayed, confused. Questioning: was it this hard for everyone, or just us? We turned to our family members, and sometimes we were greeted with "You signed up for this," or "I don't remember it being this hard."

Anything along those lines feels invalidating and unsupportive. I had no clue what I was getting myself into, no one sat me down and looked me in both my eyes and said, *You won't sleep for years. You'll lose yourself, you'll hate your partner, you'll question every decision you've ever made in your life.*

Being honest about your motherhood journey is the greatest gift you can give to another parent, and that eventually includes our children. Instead of making the hardships of motherhood fine print, we need to talk about them in headline form. The resources for help should also be printed in bold for everyone to see and benefit from.

Sometimes people confuse being honest with complaining. It's an easy mistake to make. For example, when a mom shares how many times her child woke her up last night, and that she's fucking tired, she's just stating the facts. First of all, she's allowed to be tired even if they *didn't* wake her up a million times. That's honesty. She didn't say she hated being a mother, or complained that her children are assholes (although sometimes that is also the truth), she's just having a difficult time in this phase of motherhood.

Being a mom is hard, we all know this. Talking about feelings does not mean you are complaining. Saying things are harder than you expected does not mean you are not thankful to have your children. Talking about our hardships helps normalize feelings for other moms who are going through the same thing. When you are up a million times a night, it feels like you're the only one in the world struggling.

We are not complaining about our children, but the exhausting physical and emotional pains of motherhood. **There is a difference.**

Even with all that being said, we are *still allowed to complain.* It does not take away the love and feelings we have for our children. It's okay to wish things were easier; who doesn't want that? It's always acceptable to talk about our feelings.

We complain about our jobs, hard stuff in our marriages, grocery store remodeling; it doesn't mean we want to quit, get a divorce, or never shop at our favorite grocery store again.

We are allowed to feel frustrated. Expressing those emotions not only helps us process these feelings, but can also help us find solutions.

You can still love your children and be honest about the hard shit.

You can still love being a mom and complain. Moms are talented like that.

Pretending everything is just sunshine and rainbows is toxic. It's not the other way around, I don't care what Grandma says.

YOU CAN STILL LOVE YOUR CHILDREN AND BE HONEST ABOUT THE HARD SHIT.

MOM
FRIENDS

BE
FRI

ST
END

Before I spawned offspring, I always heard about needing and wanting "mom friends," but I didn't get it. I had plenty of wonderful friends pre-children, and I told myself I was good to go.

Here's the thing about having mom friends. They understand your struggles at such a deep level that when you hang out and talk about your kids together, it's low-key (and inexpensive) therapy.

When you confess that your kid won't eat anything other than Goldfish and cheese sticks and another mom says, "Mine too," it's like the elephant standing on your chest disappears, if the elephant was made of discomfort and embarrassment.

When you compare notes about how your kids won't stay in bed either, or even when you just share recipes of what your kids will *actually* eat besides Goldfish and cheese sticks, it makes the days easier.

It's so important that there's even an app to make mom friends—it's called Peanut.

Complaining to your childless friends about the sleep you are not getting—when they willingly go out and stay out all night—doesn't really feel the same.

I'm not saying you don't need childless friends, because you do, so you can live vicariously through them and their carefree lives, and because you are more than just a mother.

But back to the amazingness of mom friends. Sitting with them at the park while your kids play is almost as good as a vacation. Being there and supporting each other through ups and downs is like making friends at hyperspeed. You go through so much together in such a short time.

YOU'RE PRACTICALLY BONDED FOR LIFE.

A friend of mine from high school gave birth to her son in the hospital room next to mine. Our children have the same birthday, and it feels like we were meant to tackle this motherhood shit together from that day forward.

When it comes to mom friends, it's nice to have people who have the same morals and ideas about motherhood, but it's not a prerequisite. No two motherhood journeys are alike, and we all experience different things at different times. The most important part of it all is that you support each other, and that's even more true when your paths look different.

WHEN SHIT GETS REAL.

There are a lot of unexpected surprises after having a child, and some of those are more bitter than sweet. Motherhood is the only part of life that completely changes everything you thought you knew but gives you little to no instruction along the way, which makes it inherently stressful.

The first step to avoiding feeling overwhelmed is to identify your triggers before stress evolves to a complete mental breakdown. You don't have to wait until you hit rock bottom to take a breather or ask for help.

FEELING OVERWHELMED CAN LOOK LIKE:

Minor Stress
1. Snapping at your loved ones—more than normal.
2. Feeling constantly tired—who am I kidding, this is our baseline most days—but even more than usual.
3. Forgetting things.

Mid-tier Stress
1. Wanting to reply, "MUST BE NICE!" anytime your partner complains.
2. Dreading your routines—again, more than normal.
3. Smiling feels weird because you haven't used those face muscles in a long time. Aka: not finding joy in the things that usually bring you joy.

Major Stress
1. Wondering what it would be like if you ran away for a week.
2. Thinking a short stay at the hospital sounds relaxing.
3. Feeling Sunday night blues, but all weekend long…

Next step is figuring out if you just need some time to yourself or need to seek professional help, whether that is therapy for you or reinforcements for your children, like an extra set of hands.

FILL YOUR CUP, MAMA

I know I need a break when I'm dreading our daily tasks and routines more than usual. Sometimes it only takes five minutes to give yourself enough of a break to recharge your batteries (okay, and sometimes it takes five days). Here are some ways to fill your own cup while you're busy refilling everyone else's.

5-Minute Ideas

- Blast your favorite songs while eating Oreos and dancing in your kitchen in your underwear.
- Light a candle and rub lotion on your hands while ignoring your children.
- Phone a friend who always makes you laugh.
- Look yourself in the mirror and say, "You're smart, you're beautiful, you're capable" loud enough until your kids think you're crazy and they eat cereal for dinner.
- Watch 5 minutes of TikTok.
- Plan a kid-free dinner with a friend so you have something to look forward to.
- Pour yourself another cup of coffee, but add whipped cream on top—trust me, you'll thank me later.

10-Minute Ideas

- Take a bath with fancy salts that have flowers in them.
- Buy an outfit for your kid-free dinner that you planned from the 5-minute section.
- Dance while cleaning something.

- Browse for a vacation online, realize the prices are too high, and be happy you didn't spend that money and stayed home.
- Do a facial, paint your nails, pluck your mustache, whatever self-grooming makes you feel pretty.
- Read this book outside while your kids try to squirt you with the hose.
- Practice yoga, work out, or do any other physical activity you enjoy.
- Buy yourself flowers or pick some from your garden.

30-Minute Ideas
- Go buy expensive coffee and wander the aisles of Target (travel time not included).
- Do a guided meditation on YouTube while lying in the comfort of your bed.
- Order dinner from Uber Eats so you don't have to cook tonight.
- Watch an episode on Netflix.
- Practice yoga, enjoy self-pleasure, work out, or do any other physical activity you enjoy.
- Ask the kids to help you clean anything so they avoid you for 30 minutes.
- Grab food with a friend.
- Nap.
- Write down in a journal all the things you are thankful for in that very moment.
- Rearrange your whole house (mentally, that is, ha ha).

If you try a handful of these and still feel like you're in free fall, it may be a good time to find professional help.

LEAVE IT TO THE PROFESSIONALS

THERAPY

1 in 7 women experience postpartum depression. PPD can happen anytime after you give birth, and there is no wrong time to need additional support as a mom.

Postpartum.net and other websites help promote awareness, prevention, and treatment of mental health issues related to childbearing in every country worldwide.

They provide book recommendations, a Perinatal Psychiatric Consult Line that you can text or call…anything you need to get the help you need.

I realized I needed therapy when venting to my friends was no longer enough, and I kept talking about the same subjects over and over again. If you're wondering whether you need help, get it. The worst that could happen is that you find out you don't need therapy, and the best is that you get the help you need and deserve.

Therapy is not a sign of weakness. It is a strength to realize when you need help.

We are not meant to do this all on our own.

If you're just looking for general therapy, I've used **BetterHelp.com** to find someone on short notice. It's an online therapy platform. You fill out an extensive questionnaire so you are partnered with the perfect therapist for you.

EXTRA SET OF HANDS

If you look at your problems, and you realize that an extra pair of hands can solve them, perhaps it's time to call in reinforcements. A lot of moms feel ashamed for needing the help of day care or a nanny, but sometimes outside care can be in the best interests of the whole family. Putting my kids in day care was one of the best decisions I made for myself and my family. I read reviews online and then chose a few to visit in person before making my final decision.

Care.com is a great place to look for help if you don't have any recommendations from friends or family.

If you're drowning in household chores, you can try the app **Thumbtack** to hire help for around the house.

Instacart is an app that delivers groceries to your door, or you can schedule them for pickup. Worth every penny not to take these crazy kids to the store.

IF YOU MUST, DIVIDE AND CONQUER

Motherhood changes every fiber of our being, and sometimes relationships do not survive this change. There's no shame in moving on. The only shame would be staying somewhere you don't feel like you belong. Like the saying goes, know when to hold them and know when to fold them.

Staying in a loveless, unhappy marriage is not going to benefit your children.

I'm not saying you should leave at the first sign of despair, because relationships are hard and they take work.

But if you do stay in a (prolonged) unhappy marriage, it will show your children that this is an acceptable example of adult relationships, and they might repeat this unhealthy pattern. It implies that they too should settle, and that being unhappy is just what happens in relationships. Do you want that for your children? I don't know about you, but I didn't carry them for nine months, give up dairy for six months, endure all the sleepless nights, and spend an eternity fetching snacks just to be miserable and do nothing about it. Don't we want our children to be happy and live fulfilling lives?

If you are going through a divorce or need support, my close friend Michelle Dempsey-Multack (known as @themichelledempsey on social media) has encouraging posts and resources to help you through this transition. This is also a good moment to seek professional help.

YOU'RE DEFINITELY NOT THE ONLY ONE

It might feel like it, but I promise anything you are going through or struggling with, you are not the only one. All of us struggle with motherhood in our own ways, and there is no one right way to go about any of this, only tools. In the end, it's up to you to trust yourself and know what's right for you. You got this, Mama.

P.S. On Reddit (online message forums at reddit.com, or use the app), you can find subreddits on almost any topic from knitting to politics. Sometimes just reading that you're not alone is enough. Just google "reddit why do my boobs look like this after breastfeeding?" and it'll pull up other people struggling with the same exact problems you are.

YOU FUCKING GOT THIS, I PROMISE

fucking

I promise

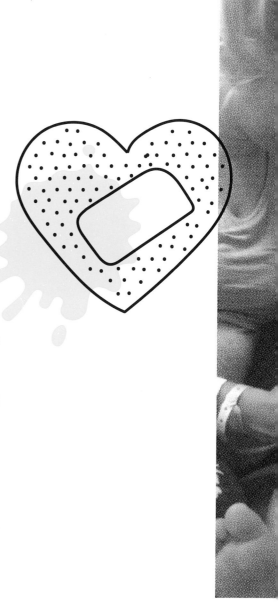

It'll feel like you've been washed away most days, but you are still there. Under the three-day-old clothes, spit-up stains, dark under-eye circles…where was I going with this? Oh yes, you are still you. This tiny human in your arms would not survive without you. Your touch and loving arms are their lifeline. Your feelings matter, your exhaustion matters, everything you do matters. Sometimes we just don't hear it enough. The voice we'd love to hear it from is just too little to tell us what a great job we're doing. This (sometimes) traumatizing period in our life is temporary.

Whether you love or hate it, it's temporary. This should be relieving to know. All the hard times will eventually dissipate…and yet so will the good.

Take the photos, Mama, and be in them, no matter what your hair looks like or how dark those circles are, because someday we will look at these photos and wish we were in that exact moment. We will long for our youth as well as our children's. Both will become great ugly-cry material as our children grow and become more independent day by day.

The good news is, it goes by fast. The bad news is, it goes by fast. Isn't motherhood such a bitch sometimes?

You fucking got this, Mama. You are the best mom for your children. You were not meant to be perfect, and neither were your children. But together you are perfect.

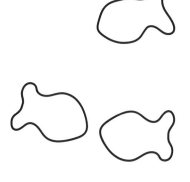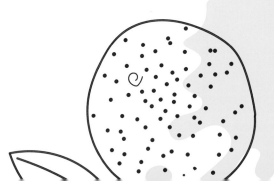

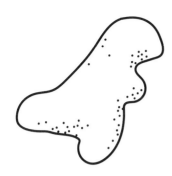

You have handled 100 percent of your worst days and you will continue to do so.

You are strong. There's no strength like a mother.

You are wise. You know your children like no one else.

You are comfort. Your children feel safe in your arms.

You are beautiful. Your eyes are your child's favorite place to look.

You are enough. You are already everything you need to be.

Nothing more, nothing less.

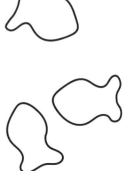

MOM LIFE RULES

When you feel down, ask for help.

Make sure you eat. Your body needs energy.

Unfollow social media accounts that make you feel bad about yourself.

Recharge. You are doing the best you can.

Motherhood is tough, but so are you.

You're allowed to fuck up. It's part of the learning curve.

You are not required to bounce back.

You might hate your partner, a little or a lot. It might go away, or it might not.

You won't want to have sex, and if you do, I'm happy for you.

Feed your baby what works best for you, from day one to eighteen years old.

Take care of yourself and seek help when you need it.

Knowing when you've reached your limit is not a weakness but a strength.

If someone gives you unsolicited parenting advice, remember it's not about you. They are reminiscing.

No matter how your child was brought into this world, you are a mother. You did a great job.

They will cry, you will cry, it doesn't mean you are doing anything wrong. It's an emotional release.

You will feel so many things in such a short period of time. You're allowed to feel tired.

Transitions are hard, but Mama, you can do hard things.

You don't have to do it all, because the list will never end.

Shush the mom guilt, practice being good to yourself.

It's never too late to be you.

Yes, you might lose yourself, but moms are the best at finding things.

The sooner you figure out what makes you happy outside of being a mom, the better. That's what is going to fill your cup. Is it singing? Painting? Dancing? Is it long walks down the aisles of Target? That is going to be your secret weapon on the days you don't see the light at the end of the tunnel. As different as all of us moms are, we still experience similar emotions, similar situations. You are never alone.

Whatever you are feeling, you are not alone.

Nothing prepares you for motherhood, and yet somehow motherhood prepares you for anything.

I promise, you fucking got this. Don't forget this is your life, too. This is the youngest all of you will ever be, so enjoy what you can and don't feel bad for the parts you can't. You know your family better than anyone (mothers-in-law included); speak up for yourself when you need to. You are setting an example for what's acceptable behavior to your children. You deserve to love the life you live. You only get this one chance to tell a story. Make it a good one.

MOMS ARE THE EPITOME OF STRENGTH, LOVE, AND RESILIENCE.

Christopher, my forever life partner, friend, and father to my children—where do I even begin? Thank you for loving me and being supportive every step of the way. I appreciate the space you gave me while I struggled and searched for myself as we worked to keep our family close and at the center of our home. I acknowledge that sharing these vulnerable parts of our lives with the world can't be easy, so thank you for letting me be me. I admire your courage.

Thank you, Elliot and Owen, for being the greatest muses in my life. I am so proud of who you are and look forward to seeing who you will become. You are so loved.

Madalin, thank you for stepping into this modern family like you've never known anything different. Watching you love my family and them love you is like rewatching my favorite movie, over and over. Thank you for encouraging me, loving me, disagreeing with me, pushing me, listening to my rants and ideas, and making me feel safe and excited about life. All these moments led me to you.

To my mom, for always loving me and supporting me. You've given me the greatest gift, which I someday hope to pass to my children: to be free of the burden to live their life to impress their parents. You let me make my own mistakes, find my own way, and express myself, and you accepted me for exactly who I am. Without your support I might not have started Fruits of Motherhood so many years ago, which led me to this very moment. I love you.

Thank you, Chia, for being a stepping-stone to trusting others to watch (and love) my kids. If it weren't for you, this book might not have seen the light of day.

A huge thank-you to my day-care center for providing a safe, educational, and caring environment for my kids to flourish while I also learned how to flourish outside of the role of mom.

Thank you to my mom friends, Brooke, Alexis, Emma, and Paula. My journey into motherhood would have been a very dark place if it weren't for your light—and by light I mean the light from my iPhone from middle-of-the-night text messages when it felt like the rest of the world was asleep and we were wide-awake. Thank you for being my hype team. Raising our children together has been amazing and raising ourselves at the same time has been extraordinary. You gave me the courage to be myself and say things that previously moms were shamed for even thinking.

Heather, thank you for believing me. Your support and guidance through this whole process have been invaluable. I can't thank you enough for helping me make this dream a reality. You're my book mom now.

Emma, your passion and excitement for writing are contagious and invigorating. I loved every minute working with you. Thank you for loving this book as if it were your own.

Thank you to everyone at Voracious. Working with you has been an incredible experience and I'm so appreciative of all the hard work you've put into helping *The Mom Life* come to life: Thea Diklich-Newell, Michael Szczerban, Craig Young, Bruce Nichols, Ben Allen, Pat Jalbert-Levine, Stacy Schuck, Jessica Chun, Katharine Myers, Mariah Dwyer, and Julianna Lee.

ABOUT THE AUTHOR

LINDA FRUITS is just your average relatable mom with a sense of humor and a big heart. Her goal has always been to make new and seasoned moms feel better about themselves through the hardest parts of motherhood. As a recovering people-pleaser, she challenges the notions of what it means to be a mother and a woman in today's world, one post at a time. She's been featured on Today.com, *Medium, Peanut, Baby Center, Scary Mommy, Parents, Honest,* and *Netflix Family,* to name a few. She is followed by numerous celebrity moms, such as Jessica Alba, Julia Stiles, and Alanis Morissette.

MY MOM LIFE JOURNAL

MY MOM LIFE JOURNAL

MY MOM LIFE JOURNAL

MY MOM LIFE JOURNAL

_____

_____

_____

_____

_____

_____

_____

_____

_____

_____

_____

_____

_____

_____

_____

_____

MY MOM LIFE JOURNAL

_____

_____

_____

_____

_____

_____

_____

_____

_____

_____

_____

_____